DEDICATION

This book is dedicated to Richard Branson, Steve Jobs, Seth Godin, J.K. Rowling, Elon Musk, Robert Kiyosaki, David Ogilvy, Al Reis, Jack Trout... the list goes on. These folks keep us inspired, keep the rope taut and remind us daily that the bar can still be raised.

D1473152

[re]wired

Selling Your AE Services
in a Post-Recession World

DAVID A. STONE

GAIL HULNICK

ISBN-13: 978-0-9939896-5-0

CONTENTS

INTRODUCTION

This is a disruptive book. It's a book that's going to encourage you to be disruptive too. To break the rules. To ignore conventional wisdom. To take a good look at the Emperor and decide for yourself if he's well dressed or not.

But it takes courage to be disruptive.

Let's face it, the AE world is not known for its revolutionaries. Nope, the practitioners here are pretty staid, conservative, law-abiding folks.

Not that there's anything wrong with staid and law-abiding. It just doesn't lend itself to revolution. And we could sure use one around here.

If the truth be told, there's a lot of mediocre marketing going on. And there's a good chance that your firm is wholeheartedly participating. What does mediocre marketing get you?

Mediocre response from clients, mediocre fees, and a plaque in the Commodity Hall of Fame.

Mediocre marketing consists of doing what you and everybody else have been doing for a long time. Websites look the same, proposals look and read the same, and presentations are pretty much interchangeable with the exception of your company logo on the slides.

We need to shake this all up. We need to embrace unconventional ideas and steal flagrantly from the leading marketing ideas outside the AE business. We need to toss conventional wisdom on its head.

But it takes courage to admit we don't have all the answers. And to admit that sometimes, the way we've been doing it simply got us to where we are today. If we want to get to somewhere else, we'd better embrace some new ideas.

As an industry, we've been looking to each other for ideas and inspiration for way too long. The inbreeding has made us all look too much alike and lowered our IQs too. Let's face it, we've learned pretty much everything there is to learn from other firms in the design professions. The next lessons have to come from outside our industry.

Marketing has become a key performance function in today's design firm. Without a high-performing marketing team—whether that team is one person or 20—that pushes you, kicking and screaming into the future, your firm simply cannot compete in the mainstream.

It's simply unrealistic today to think that your firm can successfully stand out against the crowd by touting your technical prowess and your ability to deliver a project on time and within budget. If you want to run with the big dogs you need a marketing machine that keeps you ahead of the pack.

Do you have the guts and the audacity to be extraordinary and to set your firm apart from the conforming crowd?

Taking out the Head Trash

Where can we find the guts and the audacity?

Henry Ford, one of the great innovators of the last century, once famously said, "Whether you think you can or you can't, you're right." In other words, the only obstacle to your success is your firm belief that the odds that are stacked against you are insurmountable.

Despite the delightful fact that the recession is decidedly in the rear view mirror, the world we've inherited is vastly different than the one we left behind. The rules have changed dramatically and it's making a lot of design professionals uncomfortable.

I've been hearing it every day:

"Clients don't have the same loyalty they used to!"

"The competition is red hot!"

"The big firms came to town and are eating up all the projects!"

"We've lost four great projects that should have been ours!"

It's both easy and convenient to place blame. The clients who fail to understand your value, the competitors who undercut your fees, even the planets that fail to align in your favor. Regardless of whose fault you declare it to be, when the dust has settled, the challenges remain leaving you with two choices. Give up and go home. Or find some way to climb over, knock down or bust through the wall that blocks your path.

The wall you're facing right now is called 'change.' It's the need for you to accept that the strategies and tactics that got your firm this far aren't going to get you much farther in this strange new world.

It is almost guaranteed you'll need to step outside your comfort zone. But the truth is, all growth happens at the edges of our comfort zones. Everything that's good that ever happened in your life was out of your comfort zone at some point.

I'm not asking you to jump way outside of it, but start with some baby steps. Stick your toe in the water and dare yourself to try something different.

The world doesn't look the same anymore. And isn't that great news?! Just as has been the case whenever the world has changed, there are more opportunities than problems. They just don't look like they used to. It's time to step up and decide that this exciting, strange new world is the one that you're going to conquer.

Helen Keller, a contemporary of Henry Ford's and resident of an unimaginably challenging world once said, *"Security is mostly a superstition. Life is either a daring adventure or nothing."*

Genius and power and magic

As long as we're quoting the great ones, let's hear from another.

"Whatever you do, or dream you can, begin it. Boldness has genius and power and magic in it."

Johann Wolfgang van Goethe   1749-1832

When I think back over my life so far, the things I've accomplished, the truly remarkable things of which I'm most proud, have, without fail, been those things I was most scared to do. Every one of them seemed, at the time, to be a wild and crazy idea with catastrophic consequences of failure. Every fiber of my being was telling me to run and hide under the covers, to play it safe.

But each time, something in me, perhaps that obstreperous adolescent with the twinkle in his eye and the slingshot in his back pocket who still lurks in my soul, dared me over the cliff edge. And more often than not, it worked.

Sure, I've had my share of times that I fell flat on my face in an ignominious heap. But each time I've managed to get up, dust myself off and carry on, all the wiser for my sorry splat. And the wisdom that I gained didn't keep me from trying again. Instead, it helped me refine my leap, fine tune the risk and increase the chances of success.

I've heard countless stories of men and women who, as they near the end of their lives, say that they don't regret any of the things they did. It's the things they failed to try that leave them wishing for another turn at bat.

Design professionals are trained, professional, risk avoiders. We've been shown a thousand ways that things can fail and taught to steer a wide path around the potholes. Don't get me wrong. Every time I land safely in an airplane or get to the far side of a bridge, I say a quiet one for all the right-brained designers who made sure these miraculous inventions work.

Entrepreneurs, however, are trained, professional, risk takers. They know that the best opportunities come wrapped in risk and they get up every morning looking for those opportunities, measuring those risks and excited about the possibilities they see hiding there.

There are two ways to play a game. You can play to not lose, or you can play to win.

Playing it safe, avoiding the risks, working to offend no one, is playing to not lose. In doing so we blend into that vast, featureless collection of competitors. Bland, unmemorable, easily forgotten.

Playing to win, on the other hand, requires boldness, daring and risk taking. The best coaches know that the best defense is a good offense and, unless there are only seconds left in the fourth quarter and they're up by 100 points, they don't back off.

Playing to not lose gets you second place. Playing to win gets you either first place, or dead last. Both are memorable. Both are valuable. First place wins all the marbles. Dead last pays the same as second place but comes complete with free lessons.

Don't fear failure. Fear timidity.

1

THE ESSENCE OF MARKETING

The ultimate goal of all marketing is to persuade.

To persuade groups of decision makers that your firm is worth looking at and should be at the top of their list when projects need to be done. To persuade a selection committee that your firm, above all others, is best suited to take charge of their project. To persuade a client to return and do another project with you.

Often, this need to persuade includes a need for your prospective client to actually change her mind. Maybe your firm is not the one wired to this project. She may already have someone else in mind to retain or she may believe that she doesn't need to retain anyone at all. Your job is to persuade her to change her mind and begin to believe that she must retain you.

So how does one go about persuading someone else?

Our strong left brains would love to believe that, if we simply lay out the facts, demonstrate the quality of our work and our dedication, the conclusion for any client would be obvious.

Oh, if it were only that simple!

Ethos, Pathos and Logos

Good ol' Aristotle. Can you imagine being so bright, so insightful, so influential that we'd be quoting you more than 2,300 years after you've kicked off? In any case, this old guy had some important things to say about the art of persuasion.

In his book *Rhetoric* (which was written around 350 BC and can still be bought on Amazon!) talks at length about persuasion.

> *"Persuasion is clearly a sort of demonstration, since we are most fully persuaded when we consider a thing to have been demonstrated."*

Makes sense. If you demonstrate something to me and I'm convinced the demonstration wasn't rigged or some kind of a trick, I'm likely to believe what you've told me.

Then he goes on to say,

> *"Of the modes of persuasion furnished by the spoken [or written] word there are three kinds. Persuasion is achieved by the speaker's personal character when the speech is so spoken as to make us think him credible. Secondly, persuasion may come through the hearers, when the speech stirs their emotions. Thirdly, persuasion is effected through the speech itself when we have proved a truth or*

an apparent truth by means of the persuasive arguments suitable to the case in question."

All clearly summed up in three words—ethos or ethics, pathos or empathy and logos or logic. Any attempt to persuade has to incorporate all three.

Ethos relies on your authority and honesty. If you can convince your prospective client that you are qualified or authorized to do their work, they'll give you the benefit of the doubt. That trustworthiness can be achieved with recognized credentials, a vested interest or particular knowledge or an ability to speak with obvious authority on the subject. Ethos has an intangible component too. If you don't look and act the part, you won't get in the door. But carry yourself and speak in a manner that oozes authority and you'll be given all the cred you need.

Pathos appeals to your prospective client's emotions. A touching story, a passionate delivery or a showing that you're aligned with their underlying values will get them to invest emotionally with you. Pathos can appeal in a positive way with excitement and hope, or it can induce fear by painting a decidedly unpleasant picture. Persuasion can't rely solely on pathos but without it, you're dull, flat and unappealing.

Logos uses logic and reason, backed up with facts and figures, to convince the left brain that your point is valid. This is especially important when you're trying to persuade a client about a technical issue. A purely emotional argument is going to make you look like you don't know what you're talking about, you're trying to bamboozle us, or both. On the other hand, too many technical professionals rely exclusively on logic to persuade. But it can only take you part way. If our hearts aren't in it, you're not going to convince us.

We can't begin to think about an effective marketing and sales program without including equal helpings of ethos, pathos and logos. Include those ingredients and you'll have us eating out of your hand.

'Hope' is not a reliable marketing strategy
I encounter it regularly and it usually shows up in three varieties.

The first is the declaration that, "we will become the firm of choice in our market."

That's a nice, bold statement, "the firm of choice…" And wouldn't it be grand. Clients throughout your target market, in need of the services of a design firm, having dozens from which to choose, but setting them all aside in favor of a sole source selection of you!

It's actually possible. But it requires that you provide those clients with something that is simply unavailable from any other source. Something so valuable as to be worth whatever premium you might charge. And it requires that 'our market' know and be convinced about this thing that is so valuable.

And those are the bits that are invariably missing in whatever follows that "firm of choice" statement. They never state where the value lies and they never say how they're going to get the word out to the market. Instead, they cross their fingers and hope.

The second is that firm or business unit that submits more than 100 proposals in a year and has a sub-30% hit rate. I call this the 'fling-it-at-the-wall-and-hope-something-sticks' strategy. It's kind of like walking down the street, asking random strangers if they'd like to marry you. If someone is dumb enough to accept your rather off-hand proposal, the likelihood of happily-ever-after is pretty slim.

We've long since proven that a client who doesn't know you, hasn't worked with you before and yet still selects you from a large stack of proposals does not find loyalty and value to be worthwhile traits.

Finally, there is the CEO who confidently reassures me, "We rely on word-of-mouth for our marketing."

Did you ever play the 'telephone' game around a campfire when you were a kid? You know, the one in which you pass a message around the circle and see what it's turned into by the time it comes back? Word of mouth is the marketing strategy in which you hope people say the right things about you and hope they say them often and loud enough to make an impact. It seldom works the way you'd hope.

In today's market, if you want to be the firm of choice, you have to do something to make that happen. And delivering competent service isn't enough. Everybody does that. If you merely let your services speak for themselves and fail to aggressively market, you're going to remain as one of many capable firms who wonder why they don't stand out in the crowd.

Aggressive marketing is a mandatory function in your firm today. And successful marketing demands that you have a sophisticated understanding of and facility with its principals and applications. You don't design a bridge or treatment plant and hope that it works. You've learned how, you apply that knowledge and you are confident in the results.

Marketing is equally logical and hope has no place in it.

Smoke and Mirrors

There's a dirty little secret that we marketers don't want the rest of you to know. But I'm feeling rather generous so I'm going to let you in on it: Marketing is dead simple. There is nothing complicated about it at all. It's far less complex and difficult than engineering or architecture. It's much simpler than construction. Plus, it's easy to learn and easy to execute.

There, I've let the cat out of the bag.

If it's that simple, why do so many firms struggle with marketing?

The primary reason is that we were lied to. I went all the way through architecture school where they told us that if we simply did our work well, everything else would take care of itself. Who needs to know about marketing when we're so good at what we do?!

A secondary, but still significant reason is that many firms believe that they can soldier their way to marketing success with brute force instead of knowledge. "If we simply respond to enough RFPs we're bound to win our share and be successful."

This approach ignores the simple rules of marketing and relies on hope that you are selected from an ever-expanding list of worthy competitors. As we said earlier, hope is not a strategy.

Rather than a mysterious black box, marketing success consists of knowing and following a few basic rules. If you know and follow them it works. And it works every time. If you don't know and don't follow them, you get mixed results, unpredictability and a really low return on your marketing investment.

There are just three rules of marketing.

1. What makes you special?
    What sets you apart from your competitors? What do you have that can't be found on just any street corner? What will I get from you that I can't get from anybody else? What do you have that I'd be willing to pay a premium for? If you can answer this question confidently, authoritatively and convincingly, you're well on your way to marketing success. If you can't, welcome to Commodity World!

2. What's in it for me?
    Everybody in the world has the same favorite subject—themselves. Your marketing message has to recognize and respond to that truth. Don't tell me that you've been in business since 1958. Instead, tell me that I'll benefit from almost six decades of continuous lessons-learned. Don't tell me that you've done 28 projects for other clients. Tell me that the experience you've gained will be applied to the unique challenges of my project. Don't tell me how good you are. Tell me how great my world is going to be when we're working together.

3. Over and over and over again.

    This is the easiest rule of all, but the one that's least understood and most frequently broken. What adjectives come to mind when you hear the word Nike? Apple? Disney? McDonalds? BMW? Over time, these brands have actually purchased a small piece of your mental real estate. That name recognition builds up a credibility and an equity that translates directly into sales and profits. What adjectives does your target market (note that I don't say 'clients') think of when your firm's name is mentioned? The long-term buildup of brand recognition is a fundamental requirement for successful marketing and requires consistency, regularity and patience. Those firms looking for in an instant return on effort lose interest and respond to another RFP.

Marketing is not an enigmatic black box, requiring a secret handshake and decoder ring. It's a series of simple, logical steps, taken in order and applied consistently for a predictable outcome. It doesn't make up stories, exaggerate or engage in any smoke-and-mirrors deception. When marketing is done well it simply shines a light on the reality of what you do.

But it shines a really bright light. It makes a lot of noise so that people notice and pay attention. Marketing, done well, educates, engages and excites your clients, your prospects and your entire target market. It connects with them over a long period of time so that you, too, own a small piece of their mental real estate.

Marketing is not smoke and mirrors. But nor is it simply responding to an endless parade of RFPs.

Why aren't you paid more?

I've been reading some excellent marketing books lately and came across a related passage in one that I simply have to share:

Value: The difference between the anticipated price and the marked price. If the marked price is lower than the anticipate price, the value is perceived as good. If the marked price is higher than the anticipated price, the value is perceived as poor.

Roy H. Williams, Secret Formulas of the Wizard of Ads

I hear a lot of complaining about poor fees, the constant under-cutting of prices and the lack of appreciation that clients have for the value of what you do. But we need to turn this discussion around and take responsibility.

The first thing that we need to realize is that any client who perceives that there is a value to be had from you that isn't obtainable elsewhere, will be happy to pay the higher price. This is proven day after day as stores, restaurants, businesses and yes, even design professionals across the country, charge significantly higher prices than do available alternates.

If price were the only thing, then everyone driving around out there in a Mercedes Benz would be clinically insane. Why would they pay $120,000 for four wheels and an engine, when for one fifth of that, they can have a perfectly reliable Chevy? Why would anyone eat at Chez Pierre when McDonald's has a Big Mac, Coke and fries for less than five bucks? Why? Because they perceive the difference in value for their money.

But first they have to perceive the difference and the higher value. Take 15 minutes and do a quick survey of your competitor's websites. Besides a different list of projects, do you see anything that is truly unique? Do you see anything that stands out from the crowd? Of course not! All our marketing looks and sounds the same.

Your clients need the services you sell. But when they know they can find the same thing down the street for less, they're going to go there. Your job is to communicate and then follow through on a promise that your clients get something different from you. Something worth more.

When was the last time you introduced a new service? When was the last time you adjusted the services you offer to keep in tune with, or ahead of the needs of, your clients? When was the last time you stopped offering an old service because the profit margins had slipped and you were happy to let the others fight over the meager fees? When did you last think about the various components of the services you offer and the potential for separating, repackaging, or combining them with non-traditional services to increase the perceived and actual value?

When was the last time you wondered if a different marketing approach could tell a story about the real value you offer? Not the same ol' some ol', but something different, something that really stood up and got attention. When will be the last time you complain about being underpaid?

The Big Secret of Great Marketing

There is a secret. A secret so important and so powerful that you simply MUST know it. It's the secret to fabulously successful marketing. It's the secret to tremendous wealth, sustainable success, and prolonged prosperity.

But when I tell it to you, you might find yourself a bit disappointed. Because it's one of those secrets that, once you've learned it, you'll find yourself admitting that you knew it all along. Are you ready?

The secret of great marketing is that you must find something to say that your clients would be happy to hear.

You knew this, of course. But if you're like most AE firms, you struggle to follow through when it comes to building your own great marketing strategy. The marketing that comes from most firms consists of what the firm, not its clients, wants to hear. As a result, the marketing that comes from most AE firms is predictable, identical, boring and ineffective.

Strategy is determining what it is that your client would like to hear. Tactics is determining how best to tell them. Strategy is far more difficult than tactics.

The strategy that most AE firms develop can be summed up like this: "We do good work. We've done it for a long time. We're great listeners. Hire us." If you don't believe me, take a few minutes and browse through your web site and the web sites of your major competitors. Nuf' said.

Impact in marketing is 80 percent strategy, 20 percent tactics. Good tactics cannot compensate for weak strategy. Which is why I get tired of being asked, "Should we use social media?

Should we advertise in that publication? Should we give away mugs or ball caps with our logo on them?" Your marketing fails when you pretend that clever tactics can overcome the fact that you have nothing to say that your clients want to hear.

When I work with an AE firm that wants their marketing effort to be more effective, we never start by asking what color the brochure should be or if they should put a billboard by the side of the highway. We always begin by asking what the firm has to offer that isn't available on every street corner. Far too often there's an awkward silence that follows…

So the next person who says that your marketing will be successful if you only get a Facebook page, take out an ad in my publication or sponsor my event, is lying to you. They're trying to send you somewhere you don't want or need to go.

You already know where you want to go. You want to go to the bank, to cash the checks your clients write to you. And if you offer your clients something they'd rather have than their money, they'll gladly write you all kinds of checks and say, "Thank You!" as they hand them to you.

The secret of great marketing strategy is no secret at all. It consists of identifying that thing, that valuable, unique, and irreplaceable thing that clients will get from you, that they won't ever be able to get from anyone else.

Once we've established that, the tactics are easy.

2

THE AE PROFESSIONS
IN A POST-RECESSION WORLD

My first job in this business was as a draftsman at an electrical engineering firm in Toronto in 1974. At that time, it was considered unethical to even publish a business card as an advertisement. That was unfair competition to your fellow noble professionals and you could get your wrist slapped for it.

Fast-forward to today and we've got cut-your-heart-out-with-a-rusty-knife-and-eat-it-for-breakfast levels of competition everywhere we look.

It's a different world out there. Deal with it.
In some ways it's like watching your grandfather contemplate the latest iPhone. He kind of shakes his head, mutters something about back-in-the-day and gets a wistful look in his eye as he realizes that his time has come and gone.

Here's the version of that story I hear almost daily, accompanied by the same melancholy look:

- *"We had projects walking in the door for decades with almost no marketing effort."*

- *"Our reputation was all we ever needed."*

- *"Our founder and CEO brings in all the work. Everybody loves him! He's retiring next year."*

- *"Our clients are treating us like a commodity."*

- *"None of our project managers like to sell."*

Nostalgia and sentimentality are nice, but they won't bring profitable work in your door. The recession dealt a body blow to the design industry, which was already on the ropes before it hit. This is the new normal and any firm that does not step up to the challenge of this new economic reality will go the way of your grandfather's hand-cranked phone.

Marketing—non-stop, over-the-top, aggressive and intelligent marketing—is an absolute necessity. And that doesn't mean cranking up the number of RFPs you respond to. That gets you nothing but a lower hit rate.

It means embracing a marketing and sales culture, engaging marketing professionals and learning as much about marketing as you know about engineering or architecture.

Your grandfather will manage just fine without an iPhone. But you have no choice when it comes to embracing a marketing and sales culture if you want to survive and even thrive in this game.

The bar has been raised dramatically

Last week I rented a car from Hertz. Now this isn't a particularly noteworthy event as I've done it thousands of times at just about every airport in this country. But this time I gave some thought to the car.

It was brand new with only 800 miles on the clock when I stepped into it. It was the sort of car that you see on the roads all the time but I was fascinated by what it offered. Heated seats, heated steering wheel, back up camera, satellite radio, anti-skid technology and a woman who seems to live somewhere in the dashboard and calls out directions as I find my way to the Marriott in the dark.

In other words, it was loaded with the safety, comfort and convenience features that we've come to expect in most cars today. At the risk of sounding like an old fart, I grew up in the 50's and 60's and I can't help comparing what I drive today with that '65 Pontiac that might or might not have started on a cold morning.

The bar has been raised so far that we aren't even talking about the old bar anymore.

The same applies to the AE firms we manage and rely on for our livelihoods.

Following the recession, the pent up demand caused backlogs to skyrocket and firms struggled to get the work done. Score one for the good guys!

On the other hand, clients emerged from the recession as smart, sophisticated and demanding consumers who have learned that they get to call the shots most of the time. Fees remain under pressure and competition red-hot.

In the midst of great prosperity we have tremendous challenges and great upheaval. This is exactly the kind of environment in which innovation and creativity thrive. If you're a member of the old guard it's a good time to shut up and start listening. If you're among the emerging leaders, we don't want to hear your complaints, we need to hear your ideas and your enthusiasm.

The design professions have been shaken up like never before. But disruption is a petri dish in which great new ideas are born. Here's to higher bars!

Do your clients still need a Trusted Advisor?

I mentioned a moment ago that clients have becoming unbelievably sophisticated. The recession created an over-supply of design consultants and clients have discovered that they get to call most of the shots. They're finding that they need you less and less.

On the other hand, just about every firm out there aspires to be a Trusted Advisor to their clients. This is the very definition of added value. If you can be the one to whom a client turns — regularly — for advice in situations that matter, your value soars far beyond your hourly billing rates. They know they can turn to you in the tightest of situations and count on the wisdom of your counsel. In street talk, they know you've got their back.

But in a world in which many clients have at least as much knowledge about their situation as you, and access to dozens, if not hundreds, of well-qualified providers, do they still need a trusted advisor?

I believe that clients will always need that kind of close confidante. But I also believe that design firms have fallen way behind in their ability to provide the kind of value-added advice that qualifies them as the Counselor to the King. Many firms I see barely rise above the status of 'technician-for-hire'.

While there's no question that the technical capabilities of engineering and architectural firms today are phenomenal, clients know that those kinds of skills are available anywhere. What they need instead—and often can't find—is someone who can provide wisdom and guidance on the really tough questions.

They know they need a new waste treatment plant and they know the technology options available. What they don't know, and need the trusted advisor for, is where to find the funds, how to structure the deal, how to get the bond issue passed, how to establish and pay for a sustainable operations and maintenance program, how to recruit and train operators, and how to ensure their taxpayers are getting a fair ROI.

And that's just the public sector clients. The folks on the private side already have the answers to their version of those questions. They've moved on to even tougher questions and left the selection of you to their procurement department.

The point is, trusted advisor status isn't granted to you automatically. And it's definitely not given if all you bring to the table is a nice smile and the ability to put together a great set of drawings and specs. If you can't contribute wisdom at the strategic level of decision-making, you won't (and shouldn't) be the trusted advisor.

Qualification-based selection is dead

The Brooks Act was passed in 1972. This landmark and oh-so-needed legislation required that the U.S. Federal Government (and subsequently many state and local governments) select engineering and architecture firms based upon their competency, qualifications and experience rather than by price.

Well done, Congressman Brooks!

But times have changed. In the intervening 43 years the AE profession has become much more sophisticated, proficient and amazingly capable. Whereas in 1972, there may only have been a few firms competent and qualified to properly execute a particular project, today there are way too many, fully qualified firms lining up to propose on every project.

Traditional AE marketing, the kind that's been in use since the days of the Brooks Act, promotes the firm based on its technical merits. The other day I saw an ad that a firm had placed in an industry journal that summed it up perfectly — "Our work stands for itself." This is a wonderful sentiment and there's no doubt that that firm is highly capable. But so are its competitors.

In a world in which all firms that are in reasonable contention for a project are essentially equal, we've created the economic definition of a commodity. We've come full circle back to 1972 and clients have no choice but to select on price.

So, how do you overcome the traffic jam at the top of the 'qualified' list? What do you do when qualifications alone are no longer enough?

To prevail in a world where the differences in technical qualifications and experience between firms are negligible you need to adopt a different marketing strategy that will help you stand out in a very crowded market. And I'm not above learning valuable lessons, regardless of where I find them.

In the chapter on Branding, we're going to be talking about the lessons we AE professionals can learn from people like the Kardashians and companies such as Geico. Strange sources for AE wisdom to be sure and it might make you uncomfortable or even irate.

Congressman Brooks did the industry a huge favor. But 43 years is a long time and 1972's solution doesn't work so well today and beyond. Competing and marketing based on your technical merits alone, letting your work stand for itself, are no longer enough.

There are no new clients

I recently happened to view an old photograph from the mid-1800's showing a group of pioneers trundling across the prairies in their covered wagons. So many green fields to claim! So much open space!

Not so much today. The 'green field' project is the exception as we work to recycle the old ones.

The same is true with clients. When it comes to growing your firm, there are no new clients. Every client out there today is currently being served by someone else. Now, whether they're being well served or not is another question. But you simply won't find a client who isn't already being served by one of your competitors.

That means that every new client you gain will have to be won away from an opponent. And that makes things a lot tougher. In any competition, the incumbent always has the advantage. Just ask any politician. The one who's there first has already won once, they're the proverbial 'devil you know', and they have habit and inertia on their side.

Your job to unseat them is a double challenge: Not only must you persuade the client to hire you, you have to persuade them to let the previous consultant go.

What does this mean for your marketing efforts? Once again, it means that you can't win on your merits alone. It means there's no holding back. You have to win by clearly demonstrating the overwhelming advantage of working with you.

The client wants to know what they're going to get from you that they aren't getting now. And it has to be worth the effort of switching. They won't be willing to switch, if they're simply going to end up with the same or even just slightly better skills, experience and service they have now. Your argument has to be unique, compelling, and enthusiastic.

A/E Marketing 2.0
What kind of ideas do you allow into your head?
Are they incremental or quantum?

Incremental ideas build on the past, taking the journey from A to B one step at a time. They are safe. They are predictable. They are rarely innovative or rebellious.

Quantum ideas, on the other hand, make an inexplicable leap to the next energy level. They redefine known realities and create previously unheard-of possibilities. They are risky. They are surprising. They give birth to revolution.

The marketing strategies that most design firms use have their origins in the mid 1970s. They have evolved slowly over the past 40 years but haven't changed significantly. They're based on three fundamental tactics:

1. Building reputation through word of mouth
2. Fostering long-term, trust-based relationships
3. Responding to RFPs

40 years ago—maybe even as recently as 15 years ago—these techniques served the profession well.

But the Great Recession changed everything. The post-recession world is a dramatically different place and the game we're playing today is entirely different. The rules your Daddy played by won't win this game.

Why not?

If word of mouth is so reliable, how did that unknown firm from out of town sweep in and start stealing projects that used to belong to the locals? If relationships are so important, why is client loyalty disappearing? If responding to RFPs is such a terrific strategy, why are you consistently coming second?

Yes, there are firms that are doing well now. But when you peek behind the curtain, you learn that they've implemented a whole new set of strategies. They've adopted new ways of thinking about marketing and selling their services. And they're eating everybody's lunch.

Architects and engineers are, by nature and by training, cautious folks. And when I'm driving across a bridge or standing on the 59th floor, I'm grateful for their prudence and caution. But I hate it when I see firms who struggle to stand out in a crowded field. Who feel intense pressure on their fees. Who have legitimate value to bring to clients, but can't be heard in the din.

When cautious people are in desperate need of revolution, the right answer comes in three steps:

1. Hang on to what's working and valuable
2. Toss out what's antiquated and ineffective
3. Adopt what's new and important

Real breakthroughs, the ones that change the game, can only come from a major shift in mindset. No matter how successful you already are, the jump to the next level can only take place if you allow yourself to have a different mindset. Because nothing advances until we advance how we think.

What kind of ideas do you allow into your head?

3

THE MARKETING RACETRACK

Think back. I mean way back, all the way to the 6th grade. It was field day and you were entered in a footrace. In those simple days your 'strategy' for winning that race didn't amount to much. You stood at the starting line. Someone said, 'Ready, set, go! and then you just ran as fast as you could. If you got to the finish line first, you won the ribbon.

But if you were on the track team in high school or college, or if you've ever watched the runners at the Olympics, you realize that runners at those levels employ a much more sophisticated win strategy. In essence, that strategy consists of breaking the race into a series of phases and employing running techniques that are specifically designed for success in each phase.

Out of the starting blocks they use powerful quadriceps to explode off the line. Their bodies remain low, leaning forward with pumping arms for maximum acceleration.

Once up to speed, they pace themselves around the track. They alter their stride, adjust their arm motions and change their breathing. Each runner plans her moves and knows precisely when she will attempt to overtake the leaders.

As the racers come around the final turn and head to the home stretch, tactics change again. Speed increases, strides are adjusted and breathing is modified to fuel the sprint to the finish.

As the racer lunges across the finish line, she knows victory has been decided by a few hundredths of a second. Against competition so high, the winner is determined as much by good strategy as by good legs.

The marketing and sales cycle in your company is like that Olympic race. Your competition is stiff and sophisticated. Many firms are as capable and qualified as you are, and technical qualifications aren't nearly enough to get you to the finish line.

As in the Olympics, marketing success requires strategy and finesse. The tools and tactics you use at one phase of the marketing cycle are completely different than those you should use elsewhere. Likewise, the tools designed for success in one phase are not going help you win in the others.

There are five phases in your marketing race.

Phase 1: Positioning

This is the earliest stage where you answer some very important, strategic questions.

- Who are you?
- What do you sell?
- Who do you sell it to?

And the most important question of all: Why should clients buy
from you instead of all the other firms that are selling the same
services into the same market? In other words, what sets you
apart from your competition?

To answer these strategic questions you need to assess the condition of the market, the strengths of your company, and the
state of your competition.

Are the markets you serve strong? Shrinking? Emerging? Who
are the competitors that would love to steal your clients? How
have the talents within your company changed recently?

Positioning lets you fine-tune and adjust your marketing message and strategy to respond to the changed conditions.

And don't assume that the answer to, "What do you sell?" is a
simple, "Engineering Services." Rolex doesn't sell watches. It
sells status. Starbucks doesn't sell coffee. It sells a lifestyle.

In order to determine what it is you sell, you must turn the
tables and see the world from your client's point of view. What
do they want to buy?

The State DOT employee wants to buy the comfort of knowing that you'll conform to their standards, the prestige within the department when you make them look good and the ease of knowing that you'll take this problem off their hands.

The private developer wants to buy the cash flow you'll generate by getting the project done quickly and the entrepreneurial attitude you'll bring to your decision-making.

What do you sell?

Phase 2: Brand Building

There's an old saying that goes, "If you build a better mousetrap, the world will beat a path to your door."

Unfortunately it's not true. You can have the greatest mousetrap (or engineering services) on the planet, but if no one knows about it, they won't be showing up at your door any time soon. Brand building is the phase in which you let the world know about your firm.

Most design firms don't use or understand brand building. Instead, they are 'sales-driven,' establishing and nurturing relationships with a relatively small number of clients through personal connections or business activities. These relationships often result in continued business over time, but the focus is to sell one project at a time.

While strong personal relationships are vital, relying on this method exclusively gives little control over growth and many prospective customers who may have never heard of you are missed.

The Branding Phase has three objectives:

1. Build name recognition
2. Enhance reputation
3. Build what marketers refer to as 'mind share.'

You'll notice that 'winning projects' is not on the list. That's because, at this phase in the marketing race, your goal is not to win projects, it's to become known by as many decision makers and influencers in your target market as possible.

An intelligent branding strategy inexpensively casts a large net over hundreds, even thousands, of prospective clients. Using tools such as advertising, email marketing, public relations, social media, trade shows, and other mass communication tactics will ensure they're all familiar with your name as well as the enormous benefits of hiring you.

Phase 3: Business development

Business development: The proactive development of one-to-one relationships between two people for purposes of doing business together.

From the first day you set foot in a design firm you've been told that this is a relationship-based business. Relationships are so important because your clients are making a major purchase with significant negative consequences if things go wrong.

They can't try your services out before they purchase and they can't return them for an exchange or refund if it doesn't turn out the way they wanted. They've heard you tell them it's going to go well. They've seen pictures of other projects you've done that went well. But there is no way they can prove that this project will go well until after it's finished.

The only thing they've got to rely on is the trust-based relationship they have with you. You look them in the eye, shake their hand and tell them that you'll look after their best interests on the project. And with a trust-based, personal relationship, they believe you and decide to commit to your $100,000 fee.

Connecting with your client on a technical level through your SOQ and proposal is an important step. But if you fail to connect with them on a personal and even an emotional level through business development, you don't stand a chance.

Phase 4: Sales

As your branding and business development efforts spread your name and reputation, you will come in contact with more potential clients and identify prospects with real projects that need to be executed. Once a 'hot' prospect has been identified, it's time to make your move.

The tactics in the Sales phase are far more specific and a lot more expensive than those in branding and business development. Technical proposals, qualification packages, personal calls and interviews can cost tens of thousands of dollars in the pursuit of a single project.

The smart firm does not take shots in the dark, it uses branding and business development to develop a high likelihood of success before committing to the expense of the sales effort.

Once the firm has committed however, it pulls out all the stops and develops a unique sales effort that is tailored to the precise needs of that client and that project.

Invest time and effort to carefully research the specific details of the client, the project, the circumstances surrounding the job and the competitors likely to be chasing it. Armed with this information, you can systematically prepare a proposal and presentation that are laser-targeted to this client and this project.

With a carefully planned approach to the sales phase of the race, you can regularly achieve a sales hit rate well in excess of 50%.

Phase 5: Lap Two – Customer Service and Project Delivery

Everyone has had the experience of shopping at a store that delivered such remarkable service and quality that we committed to come back again and encourage our friends to do the same.

It wasn't because the store had great advertising. Nor was it because their prices were low or that they had the products we wanted. In fact, in many cases, the stores we prefer to shop in have higher prices. We simply appreciated the level of service and attention we received at that business.

Likewise we've all experienced such wretched service that we make it a personal mission to never shop there again. Low price or product availability couldn't begin to make up for the poor service and inattentive attitude we experienced.

What is it like to shop at your engineering or architecture 'store'?

Just like the store clerk, your Receptionist, your Project Manager, your Project Engineer and everyone who comes in contact with a client has the power to bring customers back, or to send them away forever. Every action that project team members, clerical staff, executives and everyone else in your company take will influence that client to hire you again, or go elsewhere.

Even in the difficult public-sector market, where clients are often obliged to go through a formal selection process, your branding and customer service efforts can put you out front in the minds of those for whom you work. In spite of the rigorous selection procedures, public service officials have a remarkably effective way of working with those companies that serve them best.

The right tool for the job

I've always been a bit of a handyman and enjoy working with tools. Having the right assortment of hammers, screwdrivers and pliers close at hand (my favorites are the power tools that make noise and shoot flames) lets me tackle any project, confident that I have the tools to get it done. I also know many folks who really enjoy cooking and have built up a collection of utensils that are indispensible, whether they're whipping up a soufflé or a stir fry.

When marketers set out to win a steady supply of profitable work, they need a full set of tools if the job is to be done right. Many of the marketing problems that design firms encounter stem from a failure to understand which tool is appropriate for which task or simply not having the right tool available.

If you want to build brand recognition the tools you need must distribute a consistent message to a broad audience at a relatively low 'cost per touch.' Tools such as advertising, direct mail, public relations and social media are perfect for the job. If you want to convince a particular client to select you for a particular project the best tools are proposals and presentations.

Conversely, a proposal is a terrible tool to use when you're trying to build your brand. It's too focused, too expensive and too limiting. A pile driver is a bad choice for hanging a picture.

Another common mistake is when we confuse tools with strategies. Social media isn't a strategy or a plan, it's a tool that you might use to execute a strategy or plan. Depending on the plan you're trying to execute, it may or may not be the right tool.

The average workshop or kitchen contains a relatively small number of tools that can be used to build or cook up a variety of projects. But the collection always includes a few basic ones. You can't cut a board if you only have a hammer and you can't flip an omelet with a measuring cup.

Your marketing toolbox doesn't require a huge collection. But no matter how big or small your firm, how narrow or wide your market, you do need a few basics:

- You need tools to help you broadcast your brand to your entire market. Not just your current and past clients, but everyone who might ever be in need of what you sell.

- The business developers in your firm need relationship-building tools. Basic networking skills, a good command of emotional intelligence and a system to keep track of the contacts and to tickle them when the next call is due.

- The proposal writers need a strong go/no go process, a robust library of project information and a reliable, timely process for getting the information they need from the technical staff.

- The project delivery teams need a process for getting regular, reliable feedback from your clients.

It's always fun to add bells, whistles and the latest automatic electronic laser level. But to get the job done, you can go a long way with a few basic tools in your marketing toolbox. The tools are the same, what do you want to build?

Google Earth and Your Marketing Strategy

Ya gotta love Google Earth. Type in any address in the world, the little globe spins around, you plummet down and land on that street, looking at that house. Forget how useful it is; whoever came up with something this fun deserves to be filthy rich.

This cool app is also useful for explaining how the three main phases—Branding, Business Development and Sales—of your marketing strategy should be used.

Let's imagine that you plug in the Google Earth coordinates that let you zoom out to an elevation that's high enough for you to see your entire geographic footprint. Perhaps it encompasses an entire state or maybe even several. Let's call this Vantage Point A.

Within that geography, there's a collection of people who make up your target market. If your firm focuses on the municipal market you could see dozens, maybe even hundreds of towns and cities. Within each one is a Mayor, a City Engineer, a Public Works Director and other staff and elected officials.

Or, if you work in the private sector, you can see hundreds of real estate developers or commercial and industrial properties. Each one populated with key people making decisions about hiring design firms.

As you look down, you realize that some of those municipalities, institutions or companies are, or have been clients of yours already. But the vast majority of them have not. Many are clients of your competitors. Some have never had the need (yet) to hire a design firm.

Now onto this geography, I want you to impose a time horizon of two or three years. What you'd know for certain is that, from that entire geography, over the next two or three years, there's going to come a great whopping number of projects. You'd also know that your chances of winning your fair share of those projects is pretty good.

What you have no way of knowing is exactly where and from whom these projects are going to come. Most of them haven't been conceived yet. You know they're going to be out there. Just not yet.

Now zoom down so that you can see a smaller area. Maybe just one city or town within your market. And shorten that time horizon so it's set at about six to nine months. We'll call this Vantage Point B.

From here, project opportunities are starting to come into focus. Maybe there are rumors on the streets, conversations have started, some capital budgets have been set. No RFPs yet, but the picture is coming into focus.

Compared to the first vantage point there are a lot fewer project opportunities but now you know where they're likely to come from. And so do your competitors. You're still sure to win a few, but your chances of winning any given one has gone down.

Now zoom way in. To an elevation that lets you see just 10 city blocks and a time horizon of only 60 to 90 days. This is Vantage Point C.

From here you can see that there are exactly two projects, you know who the clients are, the scopes have been defined and the RFP has been sent out. Ten firms are all competing for these projects, six of which regularly keep you awake at night. Now that the picture is in sharp focus, your chances of winning one of these two projects has dropped to one in six.

What's the take-away from all this parachute jumping?

Vantage Point A is where your brand-building efforts play. Talking to the entire market, building your name recognition, enhancing your reputation, building mind share.

Vantage Point B is where your business development efforts play. Building and enhancing relationships, learning what's going on behind the scenes, connecting with the right people.

Vantage Point C is where your sales efforts—your proposals and presentations—play.

If Elevation C is as high as you ever fly, if your marketing efforts consist solely of chasing RFPs as they show up on the streets, you're doomed to a life of frustration and low hit rates. But if you've been in the game from the top, those projects will land in your lap when they're ready to touch down.

4

POSITIONING

Your firm's "position" in the marketplace refers to the way in which it is perceived by your clients, potential clients, suppliers, associates and competitors. It encompasses the services you offer, your means of delivery, the levels of service, the geographic territory you cover, your pricing structure and something vague that we might call the 'personality' of your firm.

Are you local or national? Are you high-end or bargain basement? Are you full-service, multi-discipline or focused on a specialty? Are you friendly and easy-going or straightforward and business-like?

One firm in Florida deals exclusively with the design of cable-stay bridges. Their work takes them around the world with the specialized knowledge they possess. Another firm offers general civil and survey work to the small towns and villages of upstate Pennsylvania. They are the engineering 'handyman' of the region, called upon to perform any and every type of project.

A third firm has a staff of thousands, offering full, multi-disciplinary services from multiple branch offices around the country.

Each firm occupies a particular spot within the huge spectrum of AE services available. Each firm is particularly attractive to the special needs of the clients they serve. Each firm has something unique to offer.

Factors Affecting Your Position

There are three factors that affect your position in the marketplace, only one of which you can control:

1. Your internal capabilities
2. The competition
3. The marketplace itself

Your internal capabilities

Every time you make a new hire, buy a new piece of technology, upgrade some software or learn something new, your firm's position in the market subtly shifts. If that new hire is a high profile expert, your position might shift significantly. If it's a new CAD technician the shift is smaller. Likewise, every time someone leaves your firm you also shift a bit because you've lost some of your capability.

Taken individually none of these moves typically makes a huge difference in your market position. But cumulatively, over a period of two or three years, the shift can be significant. The best firms, in an attempt to proactively control their position, plan their moves to get them where they want to go.

Let's say you want your firm to become one of the top five in the stormwater market in your state. Right now you've done some work in that area but clients don't think of you first when contemplating those projects.

You decide that, over the next three years, you're going to send two of your engineers for more intensive training in stormwater planning, acquire and master the use of the latest modeling software, hire a big name stormwater engineer from out of state and mount an aggressive branding campaign throughout the state that focuses on your stormwater expertise.

Thirty-six months from now, your firm will definitely be considered as one of the key players in that market.

The Competition

Every time one of your competitors makes a new hire, buys a new piece of technology, upgrades some software or learns something new, your firm's position in the market subtly shifts. Your position in the market is always relative to the positions of the other firms. You can't control the internal moves they make, but they affect how you're viewed.

I'm sure you've experienced a competitor moving into town, making a key hire or mounting a strong campaign. And you've witnessed how the talk about them changed as a result. Suddenly they were making waves and turning heads and you felt the consequences. While you can't control what they do, you can and must be aware of what they're doing and decide if and how you're going to respond.

Whenever Apple releases a new iPhone, Samsung and Google buy the first two, reverse engineer them, study the pricing and then decide if they need to make any changes in their own product planning. You, too, need to pay attention to what your competitors are doing because their moves affect your position.

The Marketplace

When the bottom fell out of the market in 2008, many great design firms were hugely affected. Demand dried up seemingly overnight and firms that had been at the top of their game were suddenly laying off staff as fast as they could. The firms themselves hadn't changed anything. But the changes in the market caused their positions to shift dramatically.

Your position is tied directly to market demand and you need to keep a keen eye on the status, the movements and the outlook for the markets you serve. Any big change—upwards or downwards —could have a significant impact on the position you occupy.

Let's Talk About Commodities

There is no end of wailing and gnashing of teeth when it comes to professional design fees. I bumped into it again a couple of weeks ago when a firm I was working with lost out on a project because their fee was about 80% higher than the next firm. "Why aren't clients smart enough to see value?"

It's not the client's job to see value. It's our job to show it and to provide higher value that is worth a higher price. And we're not doing a very good job of that.

A company selling a product or service that isn't common-ly available can not only charge significantly more, they can afford to provide their customers with a level of personal atten-tion that isn't feasible at low profit margins. When you stay at the Ritz Carlton, you get a 'free' doorman and 'free' turn-down service with exotic chocolates left on your pillow. The BMW dealer offers 'free' car wash whenever your car is in for service.

We're all smart enough to know that none of these frills are actually free. But the increased attention and coddling are seen as value that is added to the core product or service. Let's face it, when the lights are out and you're fast asleep (the basic rea-son you stay at a hotel), it's hard to tell the difference between the Ritz Carlton and Motel 6.

As desirable as those value-added services might be, selling a commodity service is a perfectly viable business model. When Sam Walton died, he was the richest man in America, and he became so by learning how to sell commodities. The only secret is low pricing combined with high volume. Keep your costs as low as possible, reflect those low costs in your pricing and sell a ton.

Design professionals, on the other hand, feel that their status as 'professionals,' their focus on individual projects rather than continuous process, and their strong tradition of 'doing whatev-er it takes' should be able to defeat the commodity label. Design professionals pride themselves on the service and quality they offer, rather than high volume and low price.

Unfortunately, quality and service have long since become expected by your clients. If you don't provide those, you aren't even invited to the game. In other words, they've become commodities.

If you don't want to attend the Sam Walton School of Business, here's what you must know. First, unless you offer some clear value beyond the basic service, you won't be able to sustain higher prices. Your clients simply won't pay more for a service they perceive to be available elsewhere for less.

Second, you can't offer the frills of a high-end service while charging bargain basement prices. It's simply unsustainable with profit margins that are borderline or worse.

Finally, to maintain your exclusive status, you must continuously change and update that which makes you special. Remember the law of the marketplace: as soon as you offer a unique service that can command a high profit margin, you will attract competitors. As supply increases, prices will automatically be driven down. To remain at the top of the curve, you must regularly introduce new services, features, levels of customer service or other added value. If you don't, you'll quickly slide down the well-greased, slippery slope to commodity.

Lessons from Walt Disney

Back in the 1920s a young illustrator penned a charming character that became known as Mickey Mouse. By combining the character with the emerging technologies of animation and sound, Walt Disney was the first to produce a cartoon with synchronized sound. *Steamboat Willie* was released in 1928 and was an immediate hit. Disney made good money. Then the competitors showed up.

Walt's strong entrepreneurial spirit wouldn't allow him to be one of many, so he made a really long cartoon and in 1937 audiences flocked to see Snow White and her seven dwarfs, the first full-length animated feature film. And more competitors came.

By the mid-1950s animated cartoons and movies had become commonplace, and Disney wanted more. This time he took his characters, combined them with 85 acres outside Los Angeles, and created Disneyland. While the world had plenty of cartoon characters and amusement parks, no one had ever seen a theme park before, and the profits rolled in.

Then, in 1970, with theme parks popping up around the country, Disney again stayed ahead of the pack by turning a day at the park in Anaheim into a family vacation in Orlando.

Since then Disney has continued to expand by exploring new ideas. Today it is feature film studios, cruise lines, real estate development, and all manner of profitable ventures. Continuous reinvention and creativity has kept Disney fresh, alive, and at the forefront of business success for the better part of a century.

Interestingly, Disney's business creativity not only includes new business ventures, it is equally driven by *letting go of old ideas that are no longer viable*. The last new Mickey Mouse cartoon was released in 1953!

When was the last time you introduced a new service? When was the last time you adjusted the services you offer to keep in tune with, or ahead of the needs of, your clients? When was the last time you stopped offering an old service because the profit margins had slipped and competition was too intense?

What happens to your deliverables?

Way down in the basement, behind the boiler, on a dusty shelf covered with cobwebs, lies a roll of drawings. The paper has yellowed and there are some water stains where something was spilled.

A team of dedicated professionals slaved over those drawings, perhaps for months or even years. They fretted over every line, dimension and note. And now they're lying, forgotten in a basement as the building owner, occupants and visitors enjoy the benefit of what that team created.

If you're in a building as you're reading this, stop for a moment and look around. Or look out the window at the buildings, the roads, the bridges and the rest of the amazing infrastructure that's all around you.

There were architects and engineers involved in all of it, so take a look and find the evidence that shows how hard the project manager worked to preserve the all-too-slim budget. While you're at it, see if you can see the endless revisions that the project engineer made in order to get it exactly right. And then look for the clues that tally the late nights spent to make the client's tight schedule.

Of course you can't see any of this by looking at the finished structures. Those intangibles have vaporized and disappeared. Yet those intangibles are the essence of what you sell.

The value that you provide to clients doesn't lie in that roll of drawings. It's in the power of your ideas. It's in the years of education and continuing study, the late nights, the worrying and the Ah-ha! moments in which you've miraculously created something out of nothing. Those moments in which you've turned the vapor of an idea into steel and concrete

The service you sell is utterly invisible. You can't take a photograph of 'above-and-beyond' and you can't capture 'dedication' in a box on the SF-330.

The service you sell is composed of your knowledge and wisdom, your judgment and your insight. What you sell can't be seen, touched or tasted but it has immeasurable value. Because when the project is complete and everyone's gone home, your client and the end users continue to reap the benefits of what you've done for years and years to come.

There is no shortage of clients out there who equate your services with that roll of drawings. They're wrong. But unless you let them know, in compelling, persuasive, engaging and awe-inspiring terms, about the incredible ways you make their lives easier, safer, more convenient and healthier, they'll continue to think you're the people who produce the drawings.

What do you sell?

Despite appearances, Rolex doesn't sell watches. Sure, that $25,000 thing on your wrist is capable of letting you know that it's a quarter past two. But so will the Timex that you bought at Sears for $19.95. No, Rolex doesn't sell watches. They sell prestige. While we're at it, Starbucks doesn't sell coffee; they sell a second home and a lifestyle. The University of Phoenix doesn't sell university degrees. They sell a second chance.

All of which raises the question: What do you sell?

Let's start by looking at the world from behind the desk of one of your clients: You're the mayor of a municipality that is experiencing issues with its waste treatment plant. You've been placed under a consent decree by the EPA, you're taking calls at dinner time from Mrs. McNaughton who is wondering why sewage is backing up in her basement and you're fighting an uphill battle against a tough opponent in a re-election campaign. You don't want an engineer. You want someone who will remove your stress and let you get back to kissing babies.

What if you're the Facility Manager for a pharmaceutical plant installing a new production line? You don't want an engineer, you want the peace of mind that comes from knowing that everything is going to go smoothly and you won't lose your job because you've picked the wrong provider. You not only want all personal risk removed, you want to come out looking like a hero.

There's an important message in the fact that no one ever excitedly saves up to hire the engineer or the architect. They want the end results—the clean water, the safe streets, the reduced energy costs and the commodious spaces. But the means to that end—the architect or engineer—is simply a necessary evil.

What do you say about yourself?

Most firms' websites include descriptions of the projects they've completed. The clients of those firms often talk about those projects on their websites too. And more often than not, the client's view of the project and the problem it solved, is dramatically different than the way the same project is described by the firm.

Let me give you some real examples:

The client positively gushes about the new library complex as it invites patrons to get involved with the building's ongoing performance:

> *"The Library & Event Center energy production, its energy consumption, the weather at the center and many other parameters can be viewed at the online smart building kiosk. Many of the design features that make this center a model for energy and environmental design can be viewed in the "green features" section of the kiosk."*

The firm's description, on the other hand, could put you to sleep:

> *"The complex includes approximately 20,000 SF of public library space and an additional 20,000 SF of administration offices. The library houses a collection of 150,000 books and periodicals and features a 15,000 SF multi-purpose community center and an outdoor amphitheater."*

The client describes this city park as

> *"...a picturesque swath of green to the heart of the city's arts and cultural district. The fountain, close enough for adults to touch and children to run through."*

This is enough to give you goose bumps! But the firm that designed this green oasis states simply that they provided,

> *"A fully integrated set of construction documents and coordination of the utility work and technical approvals for the project."*

The university research center sees itself as

> *"...intrinsically interdisciplinary, offering rich capabilities with exciting applications and innovations in many fields, [with] an energetic core of faculty...who are eager to collaborate."*

In stark and rather sad contrast, the firm saw their contribution as

> *"providing Civil Engineering and local Architectural consultant services including programming and design of a 97,000 sf building constructed in two phases."*

Your clients have big dreams and inspired visions and they need your help to get to the other side of that rainbow. When you talk about your work, see the project through your client's eyes. Show how you helped bring those dreams to reality and talk about the vision that you've helped realize.

The Rolex buyer doesn't really care about how well the gears and springs inside work. They take that part for granted. But they care.

5

BRANDING

Branding isn't supposed to win projects
You're breezing along the highway at 75 miles an hour when, out of the corner of your eye, you glimpse a flash of bright red and white. The images seem vaguely familiar and, though you might not actually look, your subconscious registers the colors and shapes of Coca Cola. Then, in an instant, your attention goes back to the jerk in the Camry who's self-righteously doing barely the limit in the passing lane.

What just happened? You were exposed to a brand-building moment and without your permission or even conscious awareness, it worked.

Branding is the most powerful marketing tool available to you. It has the power to position your firm as the preferred provider in your market, build loyalty, attract sole-source inquiries and significantly lower your costs of winning work.

Yet almost no one in the AE business has embraced it. Why not? Because a branding campaign will not win a project.

When Coke puts a billboard on the side of the highway they have zero expectation that you'll see it and immediately pull off at the next exit to buy a can of their sugar water.

They do expect though, that you, along with every one of the carefully-counted 318,435 drivers who pass that sign every day, will have the Coke brand brought back to the front of your mind and have that logo, those colors and that name burned even more deeply into your grey matter. Then, on a later occasion, when someone asks if you'd like a soft drink, you're more likely to say, "Sure, I'll have a Coke!" simply because that oh-so-familiar word will fall out of your mouth before any other.

A branding strategy isn't intended to sell Cokes, Camry's or design projects. Instead, it's intended to 'condition the targeted market to be positively predisposed' (in marketing-speak) to consider such a purchase when the time comes to buy.

Branding has three objectives, the first of which is to establish name recognition. They can't hire you if they don't know you exist. Introducing you once isn't enough. Real name recognition, the kind that takes hold and really sticks, takes place over a long period of time after many repetitions. How many times in your life do you suppose you've heard or seen the words "Coca Cola?"

The second objective is to enhance reputation. While it's good to know the Coke name, potential customers also need to know what it stands for. Branding repeats and reinforces the message with every 'touch' :

"15 minutes can save you 15% or more"

"The ultimate driving machine"

"Just do it"

The third objective is to establish what marketers like to call 'mind share.' Geico, BMW and Nike all own a little piece of your mental real estate. They've invested in it over a long period of time with thousands of tiny little touches through advertising, public relations, social media and all the tools in the brand-building kit. Mind share is the phenomenon that allows you to see a green lizard and think "Save 15%, or an apple with a missing bite and think "Cool."

Branding is a numbers game. It's not about talking to just your existing clients or the prospects you're following for projects. It involves talking to your entire market.

That means that ANYONE who might ever want or need your services throughout your entire geographic reach needs to hear or see your message. Because you don't have the time or the money to call on each of them individually, these broadly cast messages need communication techniques that have a low 'cost-per-touch.' A business development technique such as taking one client to lunch could cost you $150 per touch. Sending a weekly email blast to a thousand prospective clients costs fractions of a cent per touch.

Years ago I was working with an engineer and suggested that a direct mail program would be a good branding technique for his firm. He instantly nixed the idea with a dismissive, "That doesn't work! I sent out 50 letters one time and didn't get a single project from it."

Fifty letters, one time, isn't a branding effort. It's a waste of paper and postage. Nor was it supposed to win a project. But 1,000 postcards or emails, once a month for a year, a social media campaign with daily tweets, an advertising effort that regularly puts you in front of hundreds of potential clients... That's a great start to a branding program.

The Opposite of Brand

I heard it again last week: "Our clients are increasingly treating us like we're a commodity!"

Yes they are. And why shouldn't they?

The economic definition of a commodity is any product or service for which, in the perception of the buyer, the only difference between one supplier or another is price. One bushel of wheat is exactly the same as another whether it was grown on the Russian steppes or the Canadian prairies. And one Civil Engineer or Architect or Contractor is the same as another. Right?

I can feel you bristling from here!

But let's be frank, if your firm is like most, the only time a prospective client encounters you is when you respond to their RFP. Your proposal is one of many in a big stack, all competing in "The Battle of the Lists," where your list of projects is pitted against the others. Be honest, if you were a client, wouldn't you select on price too?

There is good news though. It lies in that definition when we said, "in the perception of the buyer..." While it's pretty hard to make one bushel of wheat any different from another, it's very easy to make your firm stand out from the rest as something very special indeed. But the onus is on you to communicate those differences.

The biggest opportunity you have to fight the trend towards commoditization is to proactively and aggressively build your firm's brand. It's the easiest, least expensive and most powerful marketing tool you've got.

What is your brand? It's the sum of all the perceptions and experiences that reside within the hearts and minds of clients, prospects and indeed your entire market. In other words, it's not what you are; it's what the people who do or might hire you think you are.

While the clients you actually work with have a front row seat as they develop those perceptions and experiences, the rest of the market —those people you hope will hire you in the future—can only judge you based on what they encounter in their world.

Imagine the view from behind the eyeballs of a prospective client who's not previously heard of your firm. Their exposure to you consists of a Qualifications package filled with boiler-plate, a call from a business developer who has obviously got word that you might have a project on the street and is anxious to build an instant relationship, and a proposal in response to your RFP. When a long parade of firms suddenly shows up at your door, all claiming to be uniquely qualified but all looking and sounding the same, you don't have much on which to build a really informed perception.

Brand building takes place over long periods of time. Think about the big names—Apple, Disney, American Express. They've all invested millions of dollars over many years to teach you about their companies and their products. Those branding messages are both carefully crafted and relentless. Which makes it very easy to sell you their products and services when it comes your time to buy.

But if you'd never heard of them before, they'd have a hard time convincing you that you should stand in a long line or fill out an application form before they charged you a premium for what they sell.

You can influence the perception of your buyers to where your firm is seen as something different from all the rest. A well-orchestrated branding effort that uses advertising, direct mail, public relations, social media and other select tools is an anti-commodity investment that will return many times its cost.

Your Brand is NOT...

A strong brand can help your firm grow steadily and insulate you from economic downturns. Earlier I said that your brand is the sum total of all the mental associations, good and bad, that are triggered by your company name.

But the concept of brand is still somewhat new in the design professions and there is a lot of misunderstanding. For example, I've often heard firms saying they are going to 're-brand' themselves, when in fact they're simply coming up with a new logo. Let's talk about some things that your brand is NOT.

Your Logo

Your logo (if you even have one—and there is no requirement that you do) is a visual image, intended to represent the company. Like your company name, it's the thing that is (ideally) remembered with 'positive predisposition.' That's marketing-speak for, 'they like you.' But the mental associations, good and bad, that are triggered by a logo are the same ones your customers and the marketplace have learned to connect with your company name.

The real value of a logo is the instant visual association that can be garnered with just a glance. No need to read anything. No need to take time to make sure you understand. Just a quick flash of that 'Swoosh' and we all know it's Nike and all that it stands for.

Despite all the angst that goes into developing a logo, it really doesn't matter what it looks like or what color it is, so long as you treat it consistently. Green, pink, round or square—just make sure that your target market sees the same thing over and over and over again.

Your Tagline

The same angst that is invested in logo development is also put into the creation of a company tagline. But regardless of what you write, your customers will develop their own taglines based on their assessment of your quality and performance.

A famous instance of a customer-developed tagline involved the Italian carmaker FIAT. During a period when their products were notoriously unreliable, drivers determined that FIAT stood for Fix It Again, Tony. Not what the corporate marketers had in mind!

By all means develop and use a tagline. But make sure your project quality, attention to detail, and customer service are consistent with it or your clients will develop one of their own to reflect your REAL brand.

What you say it is

As with the FIAT drivers, your brand is determined by the marketplace, not your marketing department. It is your customers who will decide what your company is best known for.

That doesn't mean you have no control. You must set out to establish your brand. But without consistent harmony between what you promise in your marketing and what you deliver in your projects, you will never control your brand.

You can launch the most aggressive brand-building campaign ever. But that brand will always be tested and confirmed by your clients. They are the ones who get to say what your brand is all about.

Permanent

Your firm today is not what it was 10 years ago. And it's not what it will be 10 years from now. As the firm evolves, so does the brand and you need to be aware of and proactive about its evolution.

Volkswagen is a very different brand today than it was when the first Beetle was introduced to the North American market in the 1960s. Likewise with Honda and Toyota. But these companies have slowly and carefully guided the transformation of their brands from cheap economy car to world-class automobile. The marketing promises have not outstripped the product quality and we consumers have been happy to let those companies guide our understanding of their brands.

It takes hard work to build and maintain a strong brand. It's assailed all the time from many sides with competitors taking pot shots, disgruntled customers or former employees raking muck and the odd black eye when delivering a project.

But it's worth all that effort. Well-known companies such as Coke and Nordstrom's count the equity of their brand as a huge plus on the balance sheet. You can get that kind of equity and value from a strong brand image too. Today would be a good day to start!

Branding Tools

Twenty years ago—even ten years ago!—the most important branding tools were advertising and word-of-mouth. Now, they are internet marketing and social media networking.

Of course, you'll still find big doses of advertising and word-of-mouth nowadays, especially online. And, in a way, social media is nothing BUT word-of-mouth, millions of terabytes of it. But the point is that it is a new landscape, when it comes to choosing the best tools to build your brand.

You'll make decisions based on your firm's priorities and characteristics, and you'll spend marketing dollars to build brand, based on your firm's budget, but the key change in this [re] wired world is that you HAVE to use the web and social media.

If you're Coca Cola or Geico, you might decide to pour millions into every one of the various branding channels: radio advertising, television advertising, print advertising, public relations and traditional media, trade shows, direct mail, sponsorships, celebrity endorsements, partnering, Web presence, and social media.

Most architecture and engineering firms are far better off if they choose and focus on a smaller number of tools. Leave out paid advertising, leave out direct mail, leave out trade shows, leave out any of the various choices—except the Web and social media.

The Web

Your website is your company's online demonstration of competence. How can you claim to be an exceptional design firm if your website looks like something from 2007? You don't have to spend tens of thousands of dollars and you don't have to take six months to update the look (or to put up your first website, if you are that far behind!—athough we'll cut you some slack if you are just starting up). Make this a top priority.

Social Media

There are some things you need to know about Twitter.

First, even though half your customers may not be tweeting, re-tweeting, friending or liking, they ARE watching, reading, and clicking. There isn't a single inquiry that comes your way that hasn't first thoroughly researched and Googled you and your firm thoroughly on the Net.

Second, I'm well aware that the average decision maker who buys your services today still remembers where he was the night the Beatles did the Ed Sullivan Show. And we both know that he ain't spending his days monitoring his Twitter feed.

But that decision maker already has one foot out the door and the other on the golf course. And it won't be long before his replacement is somebody who can tell you who is the real Slim Shady and who used to sing in Destiny's Child. In short, you need to practice and be ready for the day when Ms. Millenial is sitting in the corner office.

Third, your firm needs to recruit. Just about every firm in the country today is scouting for the next generation of talent and the ones they're hoping to land ARE following their Twitter feeds all day. Social media is the channel by which you have to be connecting to your next generation of employees, managers and owners.

Finally, Twitter and Facebook and Instagram users are more engaged with brands. The average Twitter user follows five or more brands. While you might not rack up as many followers as

YouTube, Disney and the NBA, those young professionals who are looking for their next best opportunity want to learn about your brand. And they're looking to see if you're on Twitter.

The best social media site? In our opinion, it's YouTube. YouTube is a message delivery vehicle that has yet to be maximized and its potential to grow a business is vastly greater than Facebook. The number of search strings typed into YouTube each day is second only to Google.

There were 1.46 trillion YouTube views in 2012. Let's put that in perspective: One million seconds is about 12 days. One billion seconds is nearly 32 years. One trillion seconds is 31,688 years. This means 46,264 people per second click to watch a YouTube video 24/7/365. Nearly 3 million per minute, 4 billion per day. That's 13 times the population of the United States every day.

That was 2012. The number of hours people are watching on YouTube each month is up 50% year over year

And not all those YouTube views are just a bunch of teenagers watching a hundred videos a day or retirees watching cute cat videos. While it's true that YouTube reaches 67% of the US population 18-34, it also reaches 59% of the 35-49 population, 52% of the 50-64 population and 48% of the 65+ population.

There is no 'next big thing' on the media horizon. We see only a teeming host of small and medium things. Here's one of the best of the medium things. Your Smartphone with video. Use it to collect video of customers giving you real-world, real-time testimonials 'in the moment'.

Post these testimonials on YouTube and embed them on your website. It's free. You don't even need to know what you're doing. Professional video editors are plentiful and affordable in the cloud.

And next...

The rest of these tools are for you to pick and choose, after you've put in place the two essentials mentioned above.

Direct Mail and Email

I can hear the complaints now —what's the difference between direct mail, junk mail and spam? And don't we all have enough unwelcome junk landing in our mailboxes every day?

While you may have had your fill of credit card come-on's and scratch-and-sniff perfume promotions, keep two things in mind:

1.   You get so much direct mail because the strategy works. If it weren't so successful, the flow would have stopped long ago.

2.   Your efforts don't have to resemble the Publisher's Clearing House. Yours can be a very classy campaign that reflects the professionalism of your firm.

A successful program uses a mailing list built on criteria that precisely describes your best potential customers. You then develop a series of messages that addresses the specific needs and interests of that group and show how the services you offer fulfill those needs.

What should you send? The best direct mail programs are labeled 'content marketing'. You send the prospect tips, advice or other information that they can actively use in their business or agency.

While announcements of project wins and new hires can be integrated into a program, by themselves they're of little interest to the people on your list. Instead, keep them up to date with regulatory changes, cost information, market trends, emerging technologies and cost-saving ideas.

Today's client is empowered by information. They quaff huge vats of information every day. Every decision they make, especially the ones regarding the firms they'll hire, is carefully researched. Your clients glow with pride about how well informed they are! And here's where you come in: You can and should become an integral source of that flow of information.

Content marketing is highly valuable, yet free information. With content marketing, you educate prospective clients and provide them with the information they need to know. In doing so, you become the thought leader and they come to know, like and trust you enough to do business with you.

Advertising
As we discussed previously, your objective is to own a small share of the client's mind. Sometimes, but not always, advertising in well-chosen media channels provides a great opportunity to keep your firm's name and image in front of your client group on a regular basis.

Successful advertising doesn't have to be flashy and elaborate, merely frequent and regular. Nonetheless, as with all other aspects of your branding campaign, your advertising must send a consistent message that supports the position you're attempting to establish or maintain in the market.

The best places to advertise are those media most frequented by your client group. For example, if your firm provides specialty engineering services to a niche market, money spent for advertising in a general circulation journal would be wasted. Your advertising investment would be better spent in a focused industry newsletter.

It's also important to learn the demographics of the readership or viewership of the media you're considering. You want to place ads in the media where a high percentage of readers or viewers are decision makers or those who can significantly influence a decision with respect to hiring your services.

Public Relations and Publicity
The key to any successful media release is to understand the world from the point of view of the Reporter, Editor or News Director who decides what's news and what's fluff. Their job is to sort through the mountain of information that arrives on their desk everyday and identify those items that will make it into the broadcast or the paper. To ensure your news item is included, you must first make it appealing to the Editor.

To accomplish this, a good public relations person or marketing director will get to know the Reporters, Editors and News Directors on their media list. The PR representative will visit with them and find out their policies and preferences.

Regardless of the individual Reporter, Editor or News Director's personal preference though, every one of them has the same top priority: "How does this news item affect my readers, listeners or viewers?" Unless your story shows how the readers are impacted, you'll be relegated to the back pages or the round file.

You've just hired a new Project Manager. *WHO CARES*? You've just been awarded the design commission for the new water treatment plant? *WHO CARES?* Unless you answer those questions the Editor won't run the story and the readers won't read it.

Reporters and Editors don't appreciate you getting them to run a story about your firm so you can avoid paying for advertising. Their purpose is not to help you publicize your firm.

Look for stories in your firm that allow the reporter or editor to answer "Yes!" when they ask themselves the fundamental question: "Is it news?"

When you put out a press release, make sure you are using a professional approach and are writing in the proper style. Build a solid, targeted, strategic media distribution list or hire a PR firm that can do that for you.

Etc.
Other brand-building tools to consider are trade shows, speaking opportunities at industry conferences, writing white papers and articles for professional and trade publications, sponsoring not-for-profit, sports or other organizations, hosting special events, and entering awards contests.

In every case, keep these two tips in mind:

1.   Consider the return on investment BEFORE you commit money or time

2.   Stay focused on the brand message you are putting across and make sure every tool and every activity reinforce it.

When did you last send roses?

Remember Pan Am?

Remember Compuserve?

Remember Blockbuster?

These lofty brands were once household names, yet today they're relegated to the 'whatever-happened-to…' bin. As it happens, each of these used-to-be companies went out of business for one reason or another. But the lesson for us is how quickly they fell off our radar and were replaced by Virgin Atlantic, Google, Netflix and a whole host of other competitors.

Even if a company does not go out of business, if it fails to maintain a sufficient level of visibility in the marketplace, it'll be buried by the competition. And it doesn't take long for the mental and visual space it occupied to be filled by those who want to take its place.

Think, for a moment, about all the different clients and projects you've worked with in the past five or ten years. Now think about the number of clients and projects you're working with right now—the number of active projects that are, as we used to say, 'on the boards.' My guess is that the currently active ones represent a pretty small percentage of the total. What are you doing to proactively remain 'front of mind' with all those clients who are not currently active?

It's those 'in-between' clients who are most likely to forget about you. To forget just how great it was to work with your team during the year or two that often separates their most recent project from their next. Yet it's those past clients who are the most likely, most obvious and easiest sources of profitable future work.

But if you don't maintain an active presence in the life of that client, those intervening months give your competitors plenty of time to fill the mental space that you used to occupy.

The answer is an aggressive brand-building and brand-maintaining campaign.

Tools such as advertising, direct mail, social media, public relations and a regular presence at client-oriented events such as conferences and trade shows provide a low-cost path across the field of view of all your clients—past, current and future— without the time and expense of personal visits.

When you're working on a project, you're in daily touch with the client. But between projects it can be months or even years between contacts. It's simply impossible to stay in personal touch the whole time. Monthly or even twice-monthly 'touches' via a blog, an ad in an industry journal or a mention in the media, supplemented with weekly or even twice-weekly Facebook and Twitter postings keep your name in the foreground and part of the current conversation.

Many firms try to stay in touch with once- or twice-a-year business development calls. While these visits are important, there's too much that can happen in the intervening months for you to be out of the room that long. Your competitors are lurking in the bushes, just waiting for you to leave the treasure unattended. They're all too happy to move in, take over and leave you wondering what happened.

As always, marketing is like love: leave them lonely for too long and they'll go looking for somebody new.

6

BUSINESS DEVELOPMENT

L et's talk about shopping.

You buy stuff all the time. You take your kids to the store to buy new shoes. You shop for clothes, furniture, food, sports gear and, occasionally, a new car. It's useful to understand the shopping 'process' before we can understand the role and the importance of business development.

When you need to buy a pair of shoes, a new dress or a car you go to the appropriate store and try out the various items they have for sale. You try it on, you test drive it, see if it looks good on you and if you're comfortable both in it and paying for it.

You could shop all day and not find anything that suits you. You'd go home without having spent a nickel because they don't charge you to try on shoes. But if you found some shoes, a shirt or the car that you like and you decide to buy it, then and only then do you have to part with your money.

But what if you get the shoes home and realize they don't fit quite right or you notice a flaw you hadn't seen in the store? You take them back. And the store either gives you a replacement or they give you your money back or they repair it under warranty.

When you buy stuff, your risk is very, very low. You get to try it out before you have to pay and, if it turns out that something's wrong, you get your money back, exchange it for what you really wanted or get it fixed.

Hi-Risk Shopping

Now let's look at a different situation. You're shopping for a vacation for your family. You're looking for a nice resort for a relaxing and fun-filled week. How do you try this resort out ahead of time and prove to yourself that this is going to be a great vacation?

It can't be done!

You can look on line or at brochures from the travel agent and see that the place looked great on the day they took the pictures. You can read review from other people who've been there and say they had a wonderful time. And you can talk to the sales staff at the resort and they'll all tell you how wonderful it's going to be.

Every one of these pieces of evidence is an *indicator* that your vacation is likely to be good. But none of them are proof.

Then, based on the brochures, the testimonials and the sales pitch you book the resort, buy the plane tickets, and proceed to have the worst vacation ever. It rains all week, the service is mediocre and the food is barely edible. Where do you get your vacation repaired under warranty?

You can't! You're stuck. You can complain and they'll likely apologize. They might even offer you a discount for the next time you go to their resort. But beyond that, there is no recourse. There is no safety net.

It's exactly the same when your client needs a design firm.

When your client goes shopping for AE services, they know it's the same challenge as going on a vacation, choosing a college for their kids or retaining a lawyer. Faced with this challenge, how do your clients determine that, 'Yes, this is the perfect firm for me and my project?'

There is simply no way for them to try you out ahead of time. You can provide evidence in the form of past projects, resumes and client testimonials. But these are only indicators that the project will go well. They aren't proof.

So they hire you and it goes badly. They can't get their money back. Yes, they can sue you, but then everybody loses even more. This is a high-risk decision. There's a lot at stake and a lot of intangibles to cloud-up the decision-making process.

This is a relationship-based business
This is precisely where business development comes in.

Before we go any further, let's give it a definition:

business development, *n.* The proactive cultivation of a personal, trust-based relationship between individuals who have interest and motivation to do business together.

Let's think about that client facing that high-risk decision. Make a good decision, hire the right firm and you look like a hero. But get it wrong and it's all going to be your fault. Who can live with that kind of stress?

Her selection boils down to whether or not she has trust and confidence in the company and the individuals who will be working with her to provide the service she's looking for. She's about to take a leap of faith—she's going to sign on the line based on a promise that everything will be OK.

How can your client make these intangibles a little more concrete? He does it through the quality of his relationship with you. Does he know you? Has he seen you in action in other situations? Has he seen how you make decisions? How you react under stress? Has he had a chance to evaluate your morals and ethics? Does he know that you're going to be good to your word?

This personal, one-to-one relationship is vital because at the end of the day, the only thing he's got to go on is that you've looked him in the eye, shook his hand and said, 'I'm going to look after you.' Your client can then tell himself, "Because I know and trust you, I've got confidence that you'll look after me."

That kind of confidence doesn't come from a brochure or a written proposal. It comes from a trust-based relationship between two individuals. It comes because that client knows and trusts, at a personal level, the individual who makes that promise.

The lesson here is that connecting with your clients on the technical level in a proposal or presentation isn't nearly enough. If you haven't connected with them on a personal and emotional level through your business development activities there isn't a chance that you're going to win that job.

How Does Business Development Work?

There is a great little book written some time ago titled, "All I Really Need to Know I Learned in Kindergarten." Author Robert Fulghum made the premise that life is about getting along with others and playing well together in the sandbox, all of which we learned by the age of five. We could easily adapt the title of that wisdom-filled book to, "All I Really Need to Know—*about business development*—I Learned In Kindergarten" because the secrets to success in business development are very similar to the secrets to success in life in general.

In a one-to-one business relationship both people know that success in the world of design and consulting is based on solid, trust-based relationships. The building of those relationships is the goal of business development. The simple rules of business development—of relationship building—ensure that the relationship between two business colleagues is based on the trust that is necessary for your client to comfortably and confidently prefer your firm over the others that are equally qualified.

Let's look at some fundamentals of business development that, when consistently practiced, will put you in the position of 'preferred provider' long before the selection process for a particular project ever begins.

Everybody has the same favorite subject

Everyone in the world has the same favorite subject—themselves. Perhaps it's genetic self-preservation, but all of us are self-centered to one degree or another. At some point we all want to know, 'what's in it for me?'

Singer/actor Harry Connick, Jr., tells the story about being on a film set, working with a young 14-year old actor. They were hanging out between scenes "when he looked at me and said, 'What's the secret of being popular? How do you get people to like you?'"

What a great question! And an even better question for those involved in business development.

Harry's answer? "The secret of being liked is to always ask five questions before you say anything about yourself. People won't remember what you said about yourself, but they'll always remember what you asked about them."

This is fabulous advice that we all need to practice every day. And if you doubt it's true, try this simple experiment. The next time you're at a social gathering – a neighborhood party or a business reception will do— walk up to someone you don't know, introduce yourself, and begin talking about yourself. Tell them about your job, your family, last summer's vacation, your hobbies, your favorite sports teams and your pet turtle, Ralph. Keep track of the time and see how long it takes until your new 'friend' finds an excuse to end the conversation and move on to someone more interesting than you.

Then move on to part two of the experiment. Find another person you don't know, introduce yourself and begin asking them questions about themselves. Ask about their job, what they enjoy most about it, what they find the most challenging. Ask where they went to college and how their school's football or basketball team is doing. Ask how they like to spend their leisure time. With each of these questions, be very sincere, pay close attention and ask follow-up questions whenever you can. Keep an eye on how long this conversation goes on.

You'll find that everyone else has gone home but you're still having a great conversation with your new best friend. Why? Because you spent the whole time talking about her favorite subject—herself. You shifted the conversation to put her at the center of the universe.

You were born with two ears, two eyes and one mouth and, as your mother often said, you're intended to use them in that proportion. There is far too much valuable information that we miss when we're talking. Let the other person talk. When you talk, use your time to ask questions. Lots of sincere questions that not only get you more information, but show that you're genuinely interested.

If you can't wait for the other person to finish speaking so that you can get your two cents in, you're missing a huge opportunity to build a high-quality relationship and learn some valuable information.

Career Limiting Obstacles
Your favorite pro football team has a problem. Their best place kicker—the guy with the 87% lifetime average—has retired. The scouts are working overtime, scouring every college and high school football and soccer team in the country, looking for THE ONE who will replace the legend.

The head coach's phone rings and one of the scouts is calling from somewhere in the Midwest. He's found the perfect guy— right height, right weight, amazing kicking record, great concentration under pressure, incredible accuracy. He's the real deal!

There's just one, teensy, tiny problem... A month ago he was in a terrible car accident and now has only one leg. Other than that, he's perfect!

Let's switch focus. You're a Project Manager. You graduated with top honors from the best engineering or architecture school. You can design and build anything. You're organized, efficient and productive. You're hot stuff!

There's just one, teensy, tiny problem... You really don't like doing business development. You're uncomfortable meeting people, you don't do small talk and you can't remember names. Or maybe you actually CAN do all those things, but you just don't like to.

I see and hear it all the time. And the excuses that are given are legendary. "It's just not my personality." "I'm not really a people person." "I'm much better working on projects." "I'm yer typical engineer! (chuckle, chuckle)"

We live in a wonderfully inclusive society. And thank goodness for that. We go to great efforts to ensure that there are as few barriers as possible to anyone who wants to achieve their dreams no matter what their disadvantage or disability. And more power to he and she who works hard to overcome whatever obstacles life has set in front of them.

I apologize if I'm seeming to be insensitive, but there are some limitations that we simply have to recognize as career limiting obstacles. A Project Manager who can't or won't actively engage in business development, who can't or won't bring in enough business to at least feed himself and his team is a non-starter. About as much good as a one-legged placekicker.

EVERYBODY has to make some contribution to the get-work process. And Project Managers are at the front line of that effort. The good news is that, even if you don't rate yourself as a natural business developer, you can learn to be. Yes, it will take some effort and likely some practice that will push you out of your comfort zone. But Dale Carnegie, Toastmasters and the Self-Help and Business sections of any bookstore have enough resources to turn you into a machine for selling. There are no excuses.

Somebody has to say it out loud, so I will:

If you can't or won't play an active and successful role in business development, you're not qualified to be a Project Manager. You might be a fabulous engineer or architect and we need lots of those. But if you have the title of Project Manager and aren't actively bringing in a steady supply of work from both existing and new clients, you aren't doing your job.

Any questions?

Personal Business Development Plans

So, everyone, and most especially Project Managers, Principals and Senior Staff, should be involved in business development!

That's a refrain that's been echoing around this business forever. Ever seen it happen? Didn't think so. Me neither.

The reason it never happens is two-fold: First, except for that vague platitude, there's very little instruction provided. No one ever tells 'everyone' exactly how they're supposed to be involved in business development, what their contribution ought to be and how they should balance it with their chargeable responsibilities.

Second, the general understanding is that business development consists of a lot of socializing, handshaking, small talk, lunches and general client schmoozing. I've never taken a scientific poll, but my informal research indicates that the vast majority of 'everyone' in this business would rather smack themselves with a hammer than get out there and schmooze.

Fortunately, there is a solution. I call it the Personal Business Development Plan. This approach begins by recognizing personality styles. You're familiar with that concept: The Meyers Briggs test, the DiSC profile or some other assessment tool is used to determine something you already know: Whether you're an Extrovert, Pragmatic, Analytical or Amiable. (These are my labels, every test uses its own.)

Then each person conducts a personal SWOT analysis. While SWOT (Strengths, Weaknesses, Opportunities and Threats) is typically used in business planning, there's no reason it can't be applied to an individual to determine what his or her best contribution might be.

Not all business development activities (let's expand that notion to include any activity that contributes to the 'get work' effort) involve meeting and schmoozing with strangers. A well-rounded marketing program includes research, public relations, brand-building, proposal writing, negotiation and customer service tasks, just to name a few.

Armed with the preference and aptitude information of the firm's staff and the broad spectrum of marketing and business development activities, the process becomes one of matching the right person to the right task. For example, the Extroverts might be assigned to schmoozing at the meet-and-greet receptions. The Pragmatics could look after negotiating tasks, the Analyticals can conduct market research and draft a white paper for publication and the Amiables would be naturals at customer services.

In practice it's a little more fine-grained than that. Here are some examples:

Mr. Gregarious Mixer is assigned to become actively involved in two client-based industry associations. He'll volunteer for key committees and attend at least eight monthly meetings annually. He'll have a target of meeting and launching a relationship with at least two new people each month.

Ms. Slightly Bashful agrees to attend three out of every four regular City Council meetings. She'll listen to the proceedings, become familiar with the Councilors and look for opportunities to volunteer on ad hoc committees.

Mr. Painfully Shy is going to research and write two white papers that the firm will self-publish and use as direct mailers. He'll also host a blog on the firm's website and contribute to it at least weekly.

Because each person is assigned a task for which they're suited and might even enjoy, and since everyone is only given a small, well-defined responsibility, no one ends up with a task so daunting that it cuts drastically into his or her billable time or never gets done. But by the end of the year, when everyone has done their small part, the cumulative effort and impact on your market will be huge!

What is the most important skill for business developers?

That's an easy one: The single most important skill for business developers is emotional intelligence—the ability to know and manage your own emotions and then recognize and respond appropriately to the emotional reactions of others.

Since business development is so closely tied to relationship building—an emotion-based activity if ever there was one—this is the most valuable skill you can possess.

As you interact with the world and the other people in it, you've got three vital tools: your personality, your intelligence (as measured by IQ) and your emotional intelligence (or EQ).

While personality and IQ are pretty much inherent and fixed, EQ is a skill that anyone can develop and grow.

Hundreds of thick books have been written on EQ but we'll foolishly try to summarize it in a few paragraphs.

There are two major, and four minor elements of Emotional Intelligence. Personal Competence, made up of Self Awareness and Self Management, and Social Competence, made up of Social Awareness and Relationship Management.

Self Awareness is knowing yourself as you really are. Far more than knowing you prefer action flicks over rom-coms, it's becoming aware of and comfortable with your full range of emotional reactions to the world around you.

As you become aware of your emotional responses, even the uncomfortable ones, you analyze what causes you to react in that way. Eventually you can predict your emotional response to an upcoming situation such as a business development meeting or a networking event.

Self Management is your ability to use the awareness of your emotions to actively choose how you respond. Whereas before, when you would be heading into a business development situation, you would feel fear, sweaty palms and shortness of breath, now you can anticipate that reaction and consciously choose to have a different one.

Self Management starts when you pause for a moment and remind yourself to breathe. In that moment you recall what your previous, normal response to the upcoming situation would have been, and decide that you're going to react differently this time. You take control of the self-talk that's going on in your head and turn it into positive messages of success. You visualize yourself succeeding and refuse brain-space to any negative thoughts.

Social Awareness is the ability to recognize and understand the moods and emotions of others. In this significant step beyond self-awareness, you learn to observe others and pick up clues from their body language, facial expressions, postures, tone of voice and those intangible 'vibes.'

You put yourself in the other person's shoes, empathizing what it would be like to be in the circumstances they're in. Think about the emotions—fear, anger, pride, joy—that you'd be feeling if you were them.

Relationship Management is the final step in which you imagine how you'd like to be treated or responded to in the same situation. Since it's highly likely that they'd want to be treated in a similar way, you have clues as to how you ought to behave to inspire and influence others or sort out the conflicts that arise.

There is no shortage of those who lack emotional intelligence— the overly friendly restaurant waiter who doesn't catch that you're in the middle of an important conversation, or the friend who fails to pick up on the fact that you've had a really bad day and just need a sympathetic ear.

The emotionally 'tone deaf' suck at business development.

Yes, it takes some dedication to learn and develop your EQ skills. Want a little motivation? The link between EQ and earnings is so direct that every point increase in EQ has been shown to add $1,300 to annual salary.

Nurture your network

We're a greedy lot, we humans, always looking for something for ourselves. As business developers we tend to be no better.

We build a network of friends, associates and business connections in order to feed our needs. We want leads, referrals, advice, introductions, references, tips and, most importantly, a steady supply of profitable work. You rely on your network to feed you, but what have you done lately for your network?

There is a natural human tendency to reciprocate behavior. If I do you a favor, you're motivated to return it. Without intending to sound manipulative, as business developers we can take advantage of this by planting seeds of kindness, consideration, thoughtfulness and assistance.

Your network is like an invaluable garden that produces an abundance of food—IF you tend to it regularly. But it's up to you to plant, water and fertilize it first. Only then does the garden reward your efforts.

How do you invest in your network? Start by simply staying in touch. If you only show up when there's some benefit to be gained, your network loses interest in you pretty quickly. If you're on your way to a meeting with Client A and you find yourself driving past the office of Client B, stop, stick your head in the door, and say 'Hi!' Don't try to sell anything, don't ask about future projects, just say a simple, 'I was thinking about you and wanted to say hello.' Trust me, you'll make their day!

Say 'Please.' When you're asking for anything, don't forget your manners. We tend to remember them at the dinner table but somehow forget that they're just as important in the business world. If you listen to most business conversations, you'll find that word conspicuous by its absence.

Say 'Thank you.' You can never say 'thank you' too many times. Express your gratitude for the friendships you enjoy, the assistance and guidance you're given, the revenue you depend on and the sustainability of your business because of the people with whom you work. Your mother was right: 'please' and 'thank you' really are magic words.

Pay attention to what's going on in the worlds of those in your network. Then, when you see an opportunity to help out with a lead, an introduction, a reference, a referral or even a job, jump on the chance to offer it. Even if it's nothing more than a pat on the back to lend moral support when someone is facing a challenge, the fact that you're paying attention will mean the world to them.

Give back. We spend so much time asking. Asking for a job, a lead, an introduction, valuable information. So when you've plucked a fresh, juicy tomato from your network 'garden,' make sure you return the favor. You may not always be able to return in kind, but there will always be a way for you to pay it back. I know a business developer who once arranged for some leftover lumber to be delivered to a client's son's Scout Troop so they could build a kitchen shelter for their campsite. A simple gesture, but much appreciated.

Your network of close friends and business associates is your lifeline. It feeds you work, it connects you to opportunity and it supports you when you are hurting. But a network doesn't come looking for you. You have to seek it out, develop it, pay attention to it, feed it and nurture it. Have you watered your garden lately?

Lunch With the Mayor

A few weeks back I was visiting with an engineering firm and heard an interesting story. The firm provides a variety of services to small municipalities throughout the state. They've got a great history and reputation and do pretty well for themselves. But they don't have their foot in every door and those towns where they aren't the firm of choice give them a little competitive heartburn.

This one particular burg has been working with a different engineering firm for some time now. But, like good business developers should, my guys called on the mayor and the key town council members regularly anyway. They've been keeping the embers glowing by staying in touch and letting the relationship grow.

Over the last few months they learned that not all was well between the town and its incumbent engineer. In fact, Hizzoner the Mayor was getting more than a little ticked at what he felt was less than stellar customer service and was losing patience with them. So quietly, without disparaging anyone, they spent a little more time in the town than they might have normally.

Then, a couple of weeks ago, the current engineer calls the mayor. Says he has to postpone a meeting. Again.

"That's it!", says Mr. Mayor. "I've had enough." He called my guys that afternoon and when I last spoke to them, they were scheduled to have a nice, friendly lunch with the town's key decision-maker.

Lessons to be learned:

1. Your clients are NOT committed to you for life. They're around until they decide they don't want to be anymore.

2. Business development never stops.

3. Pay attention! Ask your clients how things are going. Ask if there is anything you can do to improve your service. Never assume that all is well.

4. Waiting for the next RFP to come out so you can stampede in with all the other buffalo is a strategy for losers.

5. The little things really DO matter.

6. Just because they went to the dance with somebody else this time, doesn't mean they won't go to the dance with you next. Keep asking.

7. Taking your clients for granted is a sure way to reduce your backlog.

8. Your next new client is currently being served by one of your competitors. What are you going to do about it?

'Business Development' isn't 'Selling'

A few years back, a young (early 20's) friend and I were attending one of those 'business after hours, meet-and-greet' kinds of networking events. We were chatting together when my friend was spotted by another attendee.

Turned out this guy was a financial planner. Not the useful kind, but the kind that wants nothing but to sell you life insurance. From across the room he homed in on my friend like a guided missile, his spiel practiced and ready to launch on another mark.

"So, young man" he started, "at what age do you think a young person should begin preparing for retirement?" Now I know he was expecting to hear, "After I graduate…" or perhaps, "When I get married…" But instead what he heard was, "I've been working on mine since I was 17."

This was decidedly not what he'd anticipated and it took him a few seconds to recover from the shock of realizing that this 'mark' wasn't going to cooperate with his polished pitch. But recover he did and then went into full-throttle sales mode.

"Well, most young people might say that it's when you graduate or after you get married, but they'd be wrong!" And on, and on he went. It took us about five minutes to extract ourselves from his relentless grip. Afterwards, my friend told me that he'd never felt so desperate to get away from someone as he did in those excruciating minutes. As for the life insurance salesman, he'd come with the goal of selling and he'd failed miserably.

The very best salespeople, the most talented business developers never sell anything. That's right, they never, ever sell. They simply help people. They make lots of friends, they care for those friends and they're around when those friends need assistance. Sometimes that assistance results in money changing hands. Sometimes it's simply a generous favor. But selling? Never.

We work in an industry that provides complex, high-priced services. Those services can't be 'test driven' ahead of time and they can't be returned for a refund if things don't work out. That means that every interaction with every client must be built on the solid foundation of a trust-based relationship. The kind of relationship that takes time to launch, nurture and grow.

Too many business developers are obsessed with selling. Every meeting with a prospective client contains the unspoken (or often spoken) question: "Can I sell you something?" When I speak about business development, too many people assume I'm talking about selling. Nothing could be further from the truth.

Business development is about relationship building. Full stop.

And when you build your relationships well, nurture them for the long term and tend to them as you'd tend to a cherished friend, the selling happens all by itself.

In contrast, when you chase a prospective client with the goal of selling them your services, you might land a project. But it would be like getting one of those mail-order brides in the 1800's. Sure, you're married. But nobody's betting on the long-term prospects.

It's counter-intuitive to think that staying away from the sales process will make selling easier. But it's true. Every talented, successful business developer I've ever met agrees: Focus on the relationship and the sales will take care of themselves.

Kinda takes the pressure off, doesn't it?

Business development is like love

Remember back in high school? Remember when you were desperately in love with someone and that someone didn't even know you were on the face of the planet? What did you do?

Your high school quandary is a lot like the one you're facing now. There are people out there with whom you'd love to work, but they don't even know you exist. There are also prospects out there who know you're around but haven't recognized how talented and easy to work with you are.

Back in the high school love game, there were two schools of thought. The first group believed that love was a numbers game. If you simply asked enough people to go out with you, sooner or later someone would agree. There were two major flaws with this technique. First, it had a very high failure rate. Second, sometimes the result was a good-news/bad news situation. The good news is, you've found a date. The bad news is, it's not someone you want to spend an entire evening with!

The second school of thought took a longer-term approach to love. You spent time studying the range of available dates and targeted a particular candidate ahead of time. Then you set out to build a relationship. The first step is to get her to see that you exist: Walk by her locker every day; recruit friends to make introductions; if she enjoys music, join the band; if it's sports, try out for the team. The next was to get that first conversation. You got yourself invited to the same parties and arranged to be her lab partner. In step three you worked into expanded conversations as you sat with her at lunch in the cafeteria and arranged to 'accidentally' cross paths on the street and invite her for a coffee or soda. By this time, she's become comfortable with you, you've found some things in common and, when you ask if she'd like to go to a movie on Saturday, the likelihood of her saying, "yes" is much higher.

Life's like high school

It's remarkable how much life (and business development) is like high school. When we went to college, life was about being an expert. "Pay attention, become an expert in this narrow field, and you'll be successful." But it turns out that life is like high school. There, success was measured by how you got along with people, how much and how many people liked and trusted you and wanted you in their group.

There are a lot of highly knowledgeable experts out there and they're easy to find. Let's call them your competitors. But life and business development are like high school and we're all looking for people we can trust.

7

SALES

This chapter is a strange one. We're going to talk about what happens when there's an RFP or a project on which you want to propose. There's no question that this is the area that by far consumes more time, more money and more concern for design professionals. So we're going to give it more words, more attention and more headings and sub-headings than any other section of this book.

There are three 'sub-chapters' within Chapter 7.

7.1   Building a Game Plan
7.2   Writing the Proposal
7.3   Making Presentations

7.1   BUILDING A GAME PLAN

Step 1: Researching for a Competitive Edge

Once you've decided that the project is worth the time and money to pursue, the next step is to collect as much information about the client, the project, the selection process, the competition, and the surrounding circumstances as possible. Every bit of information you can get your hands on is valuable. It may not seem so at the time, but information is the key to success in sales and the more you have, the better position you'll be in.

In this process of investigation you want to be looking as much for the intangible things as you are for the 'hard' information. Yes, you want to find out about schedules, budgets, scopes of work and technical specifications. But you also want to learn about personalities, political winds that might be blowing, hidden agendas and alliances and all other behind-the-scenes insight that you can gather.

The more you know about your customer and their project, the better are your chances of winning. This means you must know them in depth despite their best efforts to withhold information from you. This section gives you a target list of information you should try to collect and some techniques for getting that information.

Set A Deadline!

A vital key to the research step is to give yourself a time limit. There will always be more information that you can dig up. But at some point you have to take the material you have collected, and move forward with your capture plan.

Depending on the project, your time limit might be two weeks, two days or two hours. It doesn't matter. Set the limit, dig as fast and as deep as you can, then stop and work with the material you have collected.

Aim To Discover...

About the Client

What is their business?

How does it operate?

Who are the key decision makers?

What are their overt or covert agendas?

Do different decision makers have different overt or covert agendas?

How large is the company (or agency)?

Are they growing, holding steady, or shrinking?

Who are the key people in the organization?

What are their roles?

Is there a strong 'personality' to the organization?

What is the history of the company?

What are the company's main strengths?

What are their current weaknesses?

Do you have any contacts in this organization?

Do you know anyone who has a strong connection with them?

Can you arrange an introduction with them?

Have they worked with other design firms before?

What is their level of sophistication on projects?

What are their expectations?

Do they emphasize service and quality or price?

Do we (or could we) use any of their products or services?

Do they compete with any of our other clients?

About the Project

What is the history of this project's development?

What is the project supposed to accomplish for the owners?

What is it supposed to accomplish for the users?

Does the project represent a significant step in the growth of this organization?

Does the project have any particular 'patrons' in the organization?

Does it have any enemies in the organization?

Does the project break new ground for the client or their industry?

Has a site been selected already?

If so, can you visit it?

Can you visit an existing facility and speak with the users?

How will the project be funded?

Is the funding already secured?

Are there any significant political issues or special interest groups involved with the project?

What are the design and/or technical challenges on the project?

Are their any precedents for meeting challenges of this sort?

What specialty disciplines will be needed?

Does the client already have certain people or firms in mind to supply these special needs?

About the Selection Process

How is the selection to be made?

What are the stated selection criteria?

Who has determined these selection criteria?

Do we have any reason to believe the actual selection criteria may differ from those stated?

If so, what are the real selection criteria?

What is the relative weighting of each selection point?

Are they looking for 'new and exciting' or 'standard and safe?'

Who is on the selection committee?

What do we know about each person on the committee?

What have they liked in the past?

Is there any political wrangling on the committee?

Who is in charge of the committee?

Whose opinion carries the most weight on the committee?

What is that person's opinion?

What are the expectations regarding size, sophistication and content of a proposal and interview?

Are there specific minority participation requirements for the project?

What are the required (stated) percentages as opposed to the desired (unstated) percentages?

Which are the most talented minority firms to consider working with?

Which are the most 'politically correct' minority firms to consider working with?

Does this client 'spread the work around' evenly?

If so, is it your turn?

About the Competition

What firms do you expect to compete against for this project?

Who do you expect to be the primary competition?

What services do they offer?

What are their strengths?

What are their weaknesses?

What kind of reputation do they have in the market?

Who are the partners in these firms?

What do we know about each one?

Who are their key staff members?

Which consultants do they typically work with?

What level of quality do they produce?

Are they technically adequate, competent, or superior?

Is their design work adequate, competent, or superior?

What is their present workload?

Have they won any significant awards?

Which projects are they known for?

Have they made any major blunders in the past that may still haunt them?

What is their attitude towards this project?

Where to collect all this information

That's a big list and it's highly unlikely you'll ever be able to check off every item. However, if you're sitting, scratching your head, wondering where on earth you could find out some of this information, ask yourself if you have:

Asked the client directly

Spoken with their peers

Checked with former employees

Conducted a Google search

Talked to mutual contractors or consultants

Looked in the Who's Who directory

Checked your LinkedIn contacts

Looked carefully at the stuff hanging on the walls of their office

Checked the local library

Asked a mutual client

Checked the industry association meetings or journals

Gone to the Chamber of Commerce

Collected and read their brochures and marketing materials

Received a shareholder prospectus about the company

Looked in the appropriate trade journals

Reviewed appropriate industrial directories

Read their Annual Report

Spoken with staff at the regulatory and permitting agencies

Talked with other vendors and suppliers who deal with them

Run a Dun and Bradstreet report

Some Additional Techniques

Gathering all this information can be a daunting task. But there's an entire profession dedicated to collecting and reporting hard-to-find information in very short periods of time—Investigative Journalists. The techniques they use are wonderfully effective and can serve you just as well as you attempt to get the inside story on that elusive client.

The Six Degrees of Separation

Like Will Smith in the movie of that title, journalists have always believed that it takes just six steps to connect you with any other human being on the face of the earth. It works like this:

I would like to be introduced to the Director of Facilities of the Acme Corporation. First, I have to invent a compelling reason so the people I enlist to help will be motivated to assist me.

Next, I ask someone that I know if they know someone who knows the Director of Facilities of the Acme Corporation and could introduce me. Predictably, they don't. But then I ask if they know anyone who knows anything about the Acme Corporation and might be able to put me a step closer. They remember that their neighbor down the street has a job in a similar industry. He might be of assistance.

I call the neighbor, explain how I was given his name, and ask if he knows anyone who might be able to help. He's glad to give me the name of a sales rep who regularly calls on Acme and with whom he had been dealing. I call or email that person and ask them the same question. And on it goes until I succeed in getting the introduction.

A good journalist can connect themselves to the right information source with a very few phone calls. They whittle down the number of connections by maintaining a thick file of friendly sources they have built up over the years. Your network is also extensive. (Hint: That's why you signed up with LinkedIn). You just have to start using it to collect and direct you to information.

The Scavenger Hunt
This technique is useful when you have to delegate the information gathering. It can be very effective in short periods of time. The object of the game is to see who can collect the most information in a fixed period of time.

Assign two junior staff members to the task. You can even make use of your receptionist's idle time in this exercise. Give them both a quick outline of the project, a copy of the lists from above, and explain that their task is to collect as much information about the client, the project, the competition, or anything regarding the project as they can before the time is up. Then give them a deadline. Don't make it too far in the future, a few hours or a day works fine. If they have too long a period, they will get distracted and loose focus.

Using the techniques from the Six Degrees of Separation and whatever resources they can muster, they must collect and record information. Each person has access to a phone, a computer, the library, and whatever information sources are available to the firm. Tell them that they are an ace reporter and they have a hot story due on the Six O'clock news. Then let them go at it.

The winner—the one who comes back with the most information of any sort related to the items on your list—gets dinner for two at the nicest restaurant in town.

The All Consultant's Meeting
Most clients hold an All Consultant's Meeting in which they discuss the project and answer any questions you might have. The typical approach to these meetings is that everyone sits quietly, listens to the client talk about the project and asks very few, if any questions.

Everyone's afraid to say anything in case they give away their closely guarded secrets and their competitive edge. But the net result is that every consultant leaves the meeting knowing exactly the same information as everyone else. Valuable questions are left unasked and unanswered and the client is left wondering if anyone was awake.

At your next all consultant's meeting, take a different approach. Instead of sitting quietly, go in with a long list of questions. Dominate the meeting with your questions and don't worry about giving away any 'inside information.' Ask all the questions you want. Make them insightful and challenging. Of course, don't challenge the client's integrity or intelligence, just show that you want to know everything there is to know about this project.

At the end of the meeting everyone will still walk out, all knowing the same information. (If they've been paying attention. Some won't.) But what will the client know about you? They'll know that you represent an aggressive firm who is determined to be thorough, persistent and accurate. They'll know you're different from everyone else because you took a deep and genuine interest in their project. They'll be looking forward to receiving your proposal.

Going Down The Ladder

When a client issues an RFP it usually names a contact person who will dispense the information they feel consultants require. The difficulty is this contact person will only ever give you the 'official' answers and will make sure that everyone else is also given the answers to the insightful questions you ask.

You have to find a 'back door' into the organization that will allow you to gain important insights into the company and perhaps even the project that aren't influenced by the 'company line.' The most effective way to do this is to go 'down' in the organization and speak with someone at the operations level. Someone, preferably, without a title who isn't shy about telling you what's really going on. Take the janitor to lunch. No one has ever done that before and they'll be so thrilled they'll be happy to tell you anything you want to know. And you'd be surprised at the number of conversations they overhear.

I was once helping a firm with a proposal they were writing for a multi-modal transit center in a city in North Carolina. The client was holding their cards very close to their chest and being quite uncooperative when it came to revealing insights into what was really behind the project.

I took an afternoon and visited the existing transit center where all the local buses connected. I found a supervisor whose job it was to coordinate the comings and goings of all the buses. When she went on her break I introduced myself and asked if I could buy her a cup of coffee and ask a few questions.

We had a fabulous conversation and I learned more about the project from the operations level than I ever could have by asking the official spokesperson. We were able to incorporate a lot of that information into our proposal and went on to win the job.

This 'back door' approach will almost always provide you with insight that you'll never get dealing with the 'gatekeepers.' An effective way of building lower-level connection is to have your technical staff communicate with the technical staff of the client's organization. They have a professional camaraderie which can cross corporate lines and provide you with a vital link to critical information.

But be careful not to abuse this connection. It would be risky to both your firm and the person with whom you speak.

Ignoring the rules
Despite the fact that most RFPs tell you not to speak with the members of the selection committee, it's worth considering

anyway. At the very least, call or write simply to introduce yourself, let them know you'll be submitting a proposal and are looking forward to speaking and dealing with them.

You never know, you just might gain an insight into their thoughts or feelings about the project. If someone does agree to speak with you, don't spend your time selling your firm to them. Instead, probe for their feelings. Listen carefully to what they want to talk about. Start off by asking some probing questions and then spend most of the time listening to the answers. Don't sell yourself. Instead, find out what they're thinking and worried about.

To be sure, contacting the selection committee members runs you the risk of being disqualified from the project. If that's a possibility, don't risk it. Only try this if you determine that you can make a positive impression during the conversation.

Keep a 'dossier' on your competitors
Whenever Chrysler comes out with a new model of mini-van, the first two off the line are purchased by Ford and General Motors. Why? Certainly not because they want a new vehicle. They buy them and instantly start dismantling them, reverse-engineering the systems and features of the car and doing an in-depth analysis of the pricing strategy and packaging of the vehicle. They do this because they can't survive without detailed information about the activities and strategies of their top competitors.

Neither can you.

If you want to be an effective player in the market, you've got to know what's going on with your competition. While you should not move into 'reactive' mode and make all your decisions based on what they're doing, neither can you ignore your competitors.

You should always maintain a file (let's call it a 'dossier,' it sounds so much more like James Bond!) on each of your main competitors. In it you should have a print-out of their current web site, a copy of their brochure and a list of the partners and key employees along with their outline resumes. You should also add any other pertinent information that you can discover such as key clients, project histories, known strengths and weaknesses, recent hires and those who've left the company.

While it sounds like an impossible task to gather this information, it is not as difficult as it seems. The design profession is a relatively small world. It's highly likely that someone who's working in your firm has spent time working for your competitor. Interview them. Find out why they left. Ask what's good and bad about their former employer. Your clients, contractors and sub-consultants also have information about them. They probably have a brochure lying around somewhere too. Start asking and digging and you'll be amazed at what you can find!

Don't be afraid that word will get back to the competitor that you've been asking about them — it will. But so what? Chrysler knows that Ford and GM are buying their vehicles. It's just part of doing business.

The reason you want this information is to help you get more closely wired to your clients. If you know that you're likely to go up against a certain competitor when going after a project, you can fine-tune your effort to either take advantage of a weakness or guard against a strength.

How does this work?

Let's say you've decided to chase a new water treatment plant project for a local municipality. Your research has told you that one of your main competitors has recently given a seminar at the regional APWA (American Public Works Association) conference that was very well received. This could give them a strong advantage since the local Public Works Director would be impressed with their obvious expertise. With this knowledge you might:

1.   Mount an extra effort to build on your personal relationship with the Public Works Director

2.   Conduct a short, direct mail program in which you send a series of tips on state-of-the-art treatment plant maintenance and technology to the ten Public Works Directors within a 50-mile radius.

3.   Investigate the idea of pursuing the project as a joint venture with the competitor.

4.   Look outside your area to connect with a nationally-known consultant who presented an even more impressive seminar.

There may be another strategy you choose but the point is each of these strategies acknowledges the reality of the marketplace. Without this information you'd walk in blind and then wonder why the other firm won.

The "Wired" Construction Project

I was asked to help a construction company pursue a project. It was a major renovation and reconstruction of laboratories and office buildings for a telecommunications company. The project was worth $100 million and, needless to say, was a very big deal for the company.

We did a little research on the project and the client, but, unfortunately, did not have (or take!) the time to research the competition. Everything looked reasonable but a little voice in my head kept telling me that something was odd. The client seemed to have a very close relationship with one competitor and my instinct told me the project was already wired to them. With no hard evidence however, there was no way I could talk myself or the construction company out of pursuing the project.

My client was made for this job. They were head-and-shoulders more qualified and experienced than anybody else. We put together a very impressive proposal and made the short list. We put on a blow-your-socks-off interview that went extremely well by anyone's standards. And then we waited.

Finally, after three weeks of inexplicable silence on the part of the client, they announced that, "subject to the firm putting together a team capable of running the project," the job was awarded to the competitor! No, I'd never heard that one before either.

The politics of their relationship was so strong that, despite the fact that they could not show that they could do such a big project, they were awarded it anyway!

There are three key lessons from this story. First, do your research. There are important things to be found. Second, trust your instincts. If something smells fishy, it probably is. Pay attention to your gut feeling and take the time to dig a little deeper. Finally, no matter how good you are, you'll never have a 100% hit rate. So pick yourself up, dust yourself off, and get on with your other opportunities.

Step 2: The Go/ No Go Decision
Stop Chasing Projects!

I have this recurring nightmare that haunts my sleep. In it, an itinerant design professional wanders the streets of some large and foreboding city, t-square under his arm, calling, "Project?! Project?! Has anyone got a project?!"

Occasionally, someone will toss him a project, at which point he assembles a small group who squat down on the street corner to work on it. When it's done, he gets up and begins his wandering again, looking for the next project to be dropped into his paper cup.

I always wake up with a cold sweat and a renewed determination to convince the profession that chasing projects is a really bad way to build business.

I'm constantly running into firms who assign their Marketing Coordinators to cruise the Fed Biz Ops or findrfp.com, looking for project opportunities to bid on. You might just as well pin a "Kick Me, I'm A Commodity" sign on your back and wander the streets.

Sure, there are projects to be found there. And sure, you're likely to win a few. But what has that got you? It wins you one project from a soulless client who is going to go out and low-bid the next project too. There is no loyalty, no relationships, no long-term strategy on www.lots-of-rfps.com. Scouring those sites and chasing one project at a time is like scrounging for food scraps instead of planting and tending a lush, rich vegetable garden.

The best firms, the ones who live richly off a steady supply of profitable work, don't chase projects. Instead, they always take the long view as they settle down to build and capture a market. A market that produces an abundant supply of loyal clients who want to work with them repeatedly. They invest in building their brands and their networks instead of flinging proposal after proposal at the wall, hoping something will stick.

I have hundreds of stories in which firms have spent thousands of dollars chasing after projects that were already wired to someone else, always going to be given to the low bidder, a figment of someone's imagination or came with a one-sided joke of a contract. All these, the result of chasing one project at a time instead of building a big picture strategy to win the loyalty of clients and entire markets.

Go or No Go?

I was asked to conduct a proposal-writing workshop to a firm on the West Coast. I suggested that they would get the most from the workshop if we could work with an actual RFP to which they were going to respond. We could spend the day actually writing the proposal.

When I arrived at eight o'clock that morning, the RFP was sitting on the table. I assumed they had some background so we began the discussion by me asking questions about the project.

"Who is this client?"
"It's a municipality about 20 miles away."
"Have we worked for them before?"
"No."
"Then how did we get the RFP?"
"It came in the mail."
"But how did this client decide to send it to us?"
"We don't know."
"How did this client get our name?"
"We don't know."
"Who else has been asked to respond?"
"We don't know."

By this time it was obvious the firm knew little or nothing about the client, the project, the selection process or the competition. But, as often happens, they were about to spend almost $5,000 to prepare and submit a proposal that would be nothing more than a shot in the dark. I could not go along with it.

I called for a break and went off with the marketing coordinator and a secretary to play Scavenger Hunt. They were each given a phone and ten minutes. Their assignment: find out anything and everything about this project. They began dialing.

Ten minutes later they had find out that:
• The client, a municipality about 20 miles away, was merely "thinking about" doing the project.

- The project was only a dream and no funding was in place.

- The RFP was simply intended to "kick some tires" and obtain feedback on costs to determine if they would actually be able to do the project.

- The firm was one of twelve who had been invited to submit proposals.

- The client had been given the firm's name by a sub-consultant who had also submitted the names of four other prime consultants. (Thank you very much!)

In short, they found out enough in ten minutes to decide without hesitation that the project did not warrant the effort and expense of a proposal. We reconvened and drafted a short letter of regret to the client.

The punch line to this story is that the firm's principals then told me they were glad we decided not to pursue the project because now we had time to work on another, really important proposal they had to prepare!

Should you, or shouldn't you?
How would you like to double your hit rate? Overnight?

Simple. Just cut the number of RFPs your respond to and proposals you submit in half.

All joking aside, just about every firm I've ever dealt with writes too many proposals. In a world where relationships are key, far too many firms get suckered into submitting expensive proposals that they know they have no chance of winning.

Your first step in writing a proposal that is wired to win is to stop writing ones that are likely to lose.

The trouble is the decision of whether to chase a project or not is a tough one. The one guarantee is, if you don't chase it, you won't win it. As a result, many firms shoot at anything that moves figuring that if they submit enough proposals they're bound to win some.

Unfortunately it's an expensive, time-consuming and frustrating process that often produces those good news/bad news results: the good news is you won a project. The bad news is that it's with *that* client, under those ridiculous contract terms, to design that questionable project.

Among the many advantages of cutting down the number of proposals you write is the fact that you will now have the time to invest in the proper research, writing, designing and producing a much higher quality proposal than you've ever done before. Imagine how much better your proposal will look and read when it's the only one due this Friday instead of the three that you've often had to juggle before.

Go/No Go Economics
There are also some solid financial reasons for cutting back on the number of proposals you write. Let's look at some hard numbers that ought to convince you to back off on your proposal activity.

Proposal costs vary widely depending on the size of the project, the degree of competition and the expectations of the client. But let's assume that your average cost to produce a competitive proposal is $7,500—a number that's probably close to the middle of the pack in the industry for a competitive proposal.

Let's also assume that your hit rate is 35%—and that's a little higher than average in the AE industry.

Based on these two numbers, every project that you win would have to produce a profit of $21,429 for you to just break even on the proposal costs of all the jobs you <u>didn't</u> win.

Now let's assume that you've become quite disciplined and cut way down on the number of proposals you write. Additionally, you spend more time and more money on each one—let's push it to $10,000—which increases both the quality of your proposals and the likelihood of winning.

Using this strategy, your hit rate jumps up to 80%, which isn't at all unheard of by firms using these best practices. In this case, your breakeven point falls to just $12,500—a little more than half of the previous number.

Let's recap: You cut back on the number of proposals you write, thus easing the pressure on your marketing staff, your marketing costs go down and you use the extra time and resources to raise the quality of your proposals. The result is that your hit rate and your profits both go up significantly.

If you're a fan of baseball...
No one keeps accurate score for the design professions and those who try, bump into inconsistent reporting and a desire

on the part of reportees to fudge the numbers. But it's safe to say that the industry average hit rate is somewhere between 25 and 30 percent.

Let's put that into some perspective against a group who keep score obsessively. The combined American and National League baseball batting average over the last 113 years is 0.262. That means that about three times out of four, the batter was out.

The difference between playing baseball and running a design firm is that you get to choose the pitches you want to swing at. If you don't like the look of it, let it go by. No called strikes in this business.

So let's say you decide to get really choosy about the projects you propose on. Where before you might have submitted 10 proposals, now you're only going to respond to the five best opportunities. With that move alone, your hit rate is going to go up.

Because you're not scrambling to submit so many, you've got time to do a better job on each proposal. More research. More win strategy development. More client schmoozing. As a result, the quality of your proposals goes way up, and with it, your win rate.

For an industry that prides itself on quality, accuracy and reliability, we sure drop the ball when it comes to chasing dumb project opportunities. Yes, I've heard every excuse in the book and I know that if you don't take a swing you're guaranteed not to get a hit. But when every swing can cost you $10,000 or more, it pays to be a lot more careful.

Remember, there are no called strikes in this game.

A Rational Approach to Doubling Your Hit Rate

Once you've accepted the notion that a smaller number of proposals will lead to a larger number of wins, the next step is to remove the emotion from the Go/No Go decision and make that process totally objective.

The go/no go process ensures that you're acting on solid evidence and good judgment. Using these techniques it's actually quite easy to arrive at a sensible decision. What you do after that is up to you. You may decide that you're going to go after it anyway and I have no problem with that. But at least you'll be doing it with your eyes wide open.

The go/no go decision process has three parts:

1. A "First Glance" evaluation in which you make a broad-brush decision to say "No" to the opportunity immediately or take the time to investigate it further.

2. A brief investigation into the project and the client to evaluate the opportunity in more depth.

3. A detailed go/no go evaluation process that will provide a numerical score and give you rational advice for your final decision.

The First Glance Evaluation
Go/No Go Decision Short Form
This quick assessment asks a series of key questions about the project and the client and assigns a numerical score to your simple, 'yes,' 'no' or 'I don't know' answer. The first five questions

119

address 'big' issues and the final 10 address lesser ones. You'll score points for each 'Yes' answer. But you'll get no points for each 'No.'

Big Issues

Score 10 points for each 'Yes' and 0 points for each 'No.' If your answer is 'I don't know' either score 0 points or do some research to find out.

Score/10

1	Have we done a successful project with this client before?	
2	Is the project within our defined target markets?	
3	Do we have a successful track record with this type of project?	
4	Is it likely that we will make a profit on this project?	
5	Does the client have the money to pay for our fee and the project?	

Lesser Issues

Score 5 points for each 'Yes' and 0 points for each 'No.' If your answer is 'I don't know' either score 0 points or do some research to find out.

Score/5

6	Do we have an established relationship with this client?	
7	Is there a high likelihood of future opportunities from this project or this client?	
8	Does this project have a high profile?	
9	Is the selection process fair and reasonable?	
10	Is selection based on qualifications and not low fee?	
11	Do we have the project manager, the personnel, and the time to get the work done?	
12	Is the schedule reasonable?	
13	Are we well positioned against the competition?	
14	Is the project within our established geographic region?	
15	Is the fee in excess of our minimum fee goals?	

Total Score _____

Scoring

85 - 100	This is your ideal project and you should put your best effort into pursuing it. Be careful! An, 'it's our to lose,' attitude can be a self-fulfilling prophecy.	60 - 84	It's likely you have a good chance, but so do other firms. Research the project well, make sure you are covered by a good contract, and keep your eyes open for other opportunities.
40 - 59	This is not a high priority project for you. Chase it if you want but watch your costs carefully.	< 40	Thank the client for inviting you but politely decline the opportunity. It's more trouble than it's worth.

Brief Investigation

If your initial score is high enough to warrant going further, your next step is to evaluate both the client and the RFP for clues that could help in your ultimate evaluation and in preparing your response.

Checking the RFP For Clues

There are usually clues that you can uncover by reading both the content and between the lines of the RFP that are not only useful in determining your go/no go decision, but in crafting your proposal if you do choose to chase the project. The examples that follow are all taken from actual RFPs issued by clients seeking to retain AE services.

The manner in which the RFP is written can give you insight into the project. For example:

If the RFP is written in very precise language it can be a clue that the client is ultimately going to select on price.

"The scope of work includes locking the three buildings together structurally, providing shear collectors in the floors, adding shear walls, securing parapets, securing brick veneer to structure, securing mechanical/electrical equipment, and modifying foundations under shear walls. Alternate solutions will be considered if they provide a cost savings and do not adversely affect the project schedule."

A client without much project experience may write an RFP that reflects their inexperience and ignorance of the process. This could result in either trouble as you spend time educating them, or opportunity as they pay for additional services.

"These qualifications should indicate all projects worked on during the last ten (10) years and include the name of the project, dates and specific items worked on."

An RFP that reflects a client with a great deal of project experience could spell trouble down the road and indicate the need for tough negotiations and a good contract.

"All work products of the A/E that result from this contract are the exclusive property of ABC Bank, including the right of copyright of any published work."

An RFP that is poorly written and unclear could represent a client who is in need of consulting services beyond those in the RFP. It might also indicate someone who is looking for free ideas.

"The selected firm will provide all necessary resources to complete or perform the specific duties involved in working with the Leisure Center Committee in the development of a public process to best determine the community needs for aquatic and recreation facilities."

You can often sniff out a project that is already wired to someone else when the RFP specifies selection criteria that don't seem connected to the job. There may also be a very short time frame in which to respond.

"The selected Engineering consultant shall:

- *Provide and maintain a local project office within 10 blocks of the project site.*
- *Provide a project manager who has a minimum 15 years experience on projects of this sort.*
- *Demonstrate an in-depth knowledge of the strategic planning issues that have led to the implementation of this project."*

Wired projects can also appear to have been written by someone who obviously has professional level knowledge about the project and its issues beyond what a normal client might have.

"Provide new chillers or Owner approved alternates. Repair and modify fans as required. Continue to use the existing commingled steam supply from the adjacent building. Replace the duct system in the two buildings and provide replacement in the main branch building in conjunction with the partial abatement of asbestos.

Checking the Client For Clues
While the RFP will give you clues about whether or not this project is right for you, speaking with the client will also shed light on the decision.

More often than not, especially with larger, more sophisticated clients, there's a ban on speaking with anyone except the designated spokesperson within the client's organization once the RFP hits the street. Nonetheless, you can usually judge the client's willingness to take a 'team' approach by the way they respond to your inquiries. And you definitely want to make inquiries. Too many firms base their entire response on the RFP. Make it a habit to dig as deep as you can and unearth as much information and insight as possible.

It's in your best interest to look for clients who are:

- Willing to sit down and openly discuss the project with you.

  "The City wishes to retain a firm that can demonstrate its ability to provide an effective team that will supply the City with architectural and community consultative services. The location and specific design of the leisure center have not yet been determined. The Consultant will work with the Leisure Center Committee to facilitate those decisions."

- Willing to share information about the project.

  "Please contact John Doe if more information is needed or to provide comments on this project."

  "Arrangements may be made for pre-interview inspections of the site through the primary contact person."

- Flexible about how they work with you.

  "For those invited to interview, the interview format and presentation is at the discretion of the consultant."

- Willing to let you in on information that will be helpful in your submission.

  "To assist in the preparation of the Statement of Qualifications, a draft of the Request for Proposal which defines the Scope of Work is available at the City Hall, Department of Environmental Services."

And always be wary of clients who are not interested in learning about you and your firm.

"The consultant is advised that contact with University officials regarding this project without clearance with the primary contact may lead to disqualification from the consultant selection process."

In general, always keep your eyes and ears open for clues that suggest that the client and/or the project may be easier or more difficult that it appears on the surface. Let your observations and your gut instincts influence your go/no go decision.

The Final Go/No Go Decision
It's commitment time.

Being fully honest and using all the insight you've gathered in your investigations, go through this full scale checklist to evaluate the project. Watch especially for those items marked with an '*,' indicating a potential 'deal buster.' If you answer, 'no' to any of these questions think long and hard before spending big money to pursue the project.

Go/No Go Decision Long Form
If you need a more thorough analysis of your situation and whether or not this project is right for you, try this highly detailed, Go/No Go Quiz. There are 35 questions about the client, the project and about your business considerations. Give yourself one point for each 'Yes' answer and zero points for each 'No' or 'Don't Know' answer. As you go through this full-scale checklist be fully honest with yourself. While it's really easy to 'game' this system, lack of honesty will only hurt you and your success.

About the Client

	Issue	Y	N	DK
1	Have we dealt with this client before?			
2	Do we know that this client is financially stable and has a good business reputation?			
3	Does this client pay their bills promptly?			
4	Is this the type of project the client has worked on before both successfully and regularly?			
5	Is the client willing to spend the necessary time with you to fully discuss the project prior to preparing the proposal?			
6	Are there future opportunities with this client?			
7	Do we know who makes the final decision?			

8	Would our other clients approve of our involvement with this project?			
9	Is the client realistic about schedule and budget?			

About the Project

	Issue	Y	N	DK
10	Is there a well defined scope of work?			
11	Will the permits and approvals be obtainable within the schedule?			
12	Are we familiar with all the applicable regulations and technologies?			
13	Are there future opportunities for similar projects with other clients?			
14	Is this the type of project we've worked on before both successfully and regularly?			
15	Do we have a project manager experienced with this type of project?			
16	Are we sure our work load will not be strained by taking on this project now?			
17	Do we have at least as much chance to be selected as our competitors?			
18	Can we comply with the schedule for completing our portion of the work?			
19	Can we provide high quality client service?			

Your Business Considerations

	Issue	Y	N	DK
20	Is this what our business and marketing plans say we should be doing?			
21	Is the selection process reasonable?			
22	Do we have a strong message that will differentiate us from the competition?			
23	Will the project be worth the marketing effort it takes to get it?			
24	Can we comply with any MBE, WBE, DBE requirements?			
25	Will the contract sufficiently limit our liability?			
26	Will the contract be equitable?			
27	Will the contract be free of hold-harmless and indemnity provisions?			
28	Will the contract be free of speculative aspects?			
29	Will our fee be adequate? Profitable?			
30	Is there a good reason to take this job if we don't anticipate a profit?			
31	Will our fee be competitive?			
32	Is the owner willing to fund unexpected contingencies?			

33	Have we checked the insurance requirements and found there are no special insurance needs?			
34	Is this a project in which we should be investing our resources?			
35	Is this the best opportunity we have now?			

Total Score _____

Scoring: Count up your 'Yes' answers.

30 or more	Go for it with all you've got
25 – 30	Think this through again
20 – 24	Look for another opportunity
< 20	Turn down the project

What if we're wrong?
I heard an absolutely outrageous proposition the other day.

I was conducting a two-day proposal and presentation workshop for one of my favorite clients. We were having a pretty intense discussion about the go/no go decision-making process and abysmal hit rates when the CEO posed a truly radical notion:

"What if you were accountable for your hit rate?"

There was a whole lot of silence in the room.

Most firms have some sort of go/no go decision-making process, some more formal than others. But I've yet to see any system that isn't regularly gamed to allow the project manager or
business unit leader to do what they'd already made up their
minds to do regardless.

Standard industry practice is to throw proposals against the
wall until something sticks. Statistically, less than a third of
them do.

But what if you were accountable for that hit rate? What if part
of your annual evaluation looked at the amount of time and
money you wasted chasing those proverbial wild geese? What
if the project manager who went after 10 projects and won three
got less than half the bonus of the one who went after just five
but won four?

The average cost of a competitive proposal today varies wild-
ly, but let's say it's around $10,000. If your hit rate is 25%, the
break-even point of the winning projects in order to cover the
cost of the losers is:

$10,000 ÷ 25% = $40,000

A project manager who doubles their hit rate to 50% saves the
firm $20k and could put forth a reasonable claim for a piece of
those savings.

Absolutely outrageous? On reflection, it might just be a stroke
of genius.

Step 3: Developing a Win Strategy

Now that you've gathered as much information as possible about the project, the client and the competition you're almost ready to prepare and launch the win strategy in earnest.

The premise of the vast majority of capture plans is:

"If I give you enough information about myself, my firm and what we have done for others, you will be able to extrapolate and make assumptions about what we can do for you."

Unfortunately, potential clients (in their role as ego-centric human beings) get tired of reading and hearing about you and want to hear more about themselves. They will usually give up reading about you because they lose interest. Besides, reading about you is just like reading about every other consultant in the pile of proposals. Every proposal has long lists of projects. Each proposal has very similar-looking resumes. Every proposal states that the firm is uniquely qualified.

Wouldn't you get tired of reading this stuff?

How then, can you craft a message that not only keeps the client's interest, but actually convinces them that they should hire you? It's not as difficult as you might think.

This next step is not likely one you've commonly taken. While it might be unusual, it's not terribly difficult and it is by far the most critical to crafting an effective capture plan.

The Brainstorming Session

For this critical exercise you must gather the key members of the project team into a room for a short brainstorming session. It should take no more than one hour, but I can't overemphasize the importance of this meeting.

Who should be present?

- The principal who is responsible for the client.

- The marketing person who has been following the effort.

- The project manager who will likely take the project through to completion.

- Any key staff members who will be involved with the project.

- Anyone else who may have additional information and insight into the client and the project.

In some cases, this long list will add up to just one person. In others, it might be four or five people. Regardless, gather this group and let's get them thinking.

The purpose of this exercise is to first step outside of the normal process of writing standard sections in a proposal. Then to step into the key issues that the client will consider when choosing the consultant for their project.

Your answers to these questions will serve as the themes that run throughout your business development effort and ensure that it is written in direct response to the client's agenda and their needs. In short, it will wire you to the client and the project.

The Brainstorming Questions

In this exercise you're going to answer five very important questions. Refer to the information you have dug up during your research to ensure your answers are accurate and not simply 'gut feel.'

When you're done, the answers will serve as the themes that run through your proposal and tie it directly to the client's biggest concerns about this project.

Question #1: *In the mind of the client what are the 'hot buttons' on this project?*
Hot buttons are those key, pivotal issues that the key decision makers will consider the most important in the execution of this project.

Hot buttons come in many 'flavors.' On one project the overriding issue might be budget. The client must complete the project for as little cost as possible. On another it might be schedule since a looming deadline makes on-time completion of the project imperative. A third project may be driven by political issues where an incumbent candidate depends on its successful completion as a major plank in an election campaign. And on yet another project the key issues may be technical or design related.

While there is often a single overriding issue that dominates the others, there is rarely only one hot button. Your job is to identify all the hot buttons that are driving this particular project. List as many as you can think of then, if there are sufficient, prioritize them into the top five.

Write your answers and a flip chart sheet and hang it on the wall.

Example
The project was to reconstruct a bridge that crossed a toll highway. The existing bridge was old and beyond repair. The problem was that the toll highway had been built between the residential and the business sections of town. With the bridge out of commission during construction, the only way to the business district was a three-mile detour. It was faster and more convenient to simply go to the business district of the next town. Business owners were furious about the project.

Key Hot Buttons on this project

1.   Schedule: Get the old bridge down and the new bridge up and open in as little time as possible.

2.   Community Relations: Keep the businesses as informed as possible through this unfortunate process. If they feel they are in the dark, they will react very negatively. At the same time, try to keep the detour route as convenient as possible to keep traffic going to the main business district.

3.   Keep traffic flowing on the toll highway: Although construction is going on above, closing the toll road is not an option.

While there were some additional, secondary 'hot buttons' on this actual project, these three were by far the most important for success. You'll notice that budget was not included in the key list. Nor were there any technical issues regarding design or construction of the bridge. In this case the bridge itself was quite straightforward and simple. Virtually any competent bridge engineer could easily design it.

So the firm that pursues this project by touting its strong technical capability and listing all the bridges they had designed would miss the point completely.

Question #2: What are the traits of the 'perfect firm' for this project? Here's the situation: You are the key decision maker in the client's organization. You are responsible for choosing the consultant to be used on this project. It's about 5:00 AM and you're lying in bed, half asleep, half awake.

You're dreaming about the project and the consultant you'll hire. You're not thinking about any particular consultant. Instead, your dream has invented the perfect consultant, the one you would hire in a heartbeat if they existed outside your dream. What is that firm like?

Write your answers and a flip chart sheet and hang it on the wall.

Example
Let's look at the key decision-makers for two completely different clients.

"A" is a 48-year old State DOT employee. He's worked for the state his entire career and has risen to an upper management position. His pension is fully vested and he'd like to move up two more steps in the ladder before taking early retirement. This project is his 'baby' and he's been nursing it through the system for two years. If it goes well, he'll likely be given his next promotion.

What would the firm of his dreams look like?

1. They'd work hard to make him look good to his superiors.

2. They'd thoroughly understand and work within the department's bureaucratic process.

3. They'd be a known entity that had been tried and tested on previous projects. No one could criticize such a safe choice.

"B" is a 35-year old shopping center developer. This woman is self-made and pushes herself and everyone around her very hard. She is always looking for a better deal and a faster way to get things done. As she drives around in her BMW she has Bluetooth headsets on each ear and a fax machine in the back seat on which she is permanently making deals. What is her 'ideal firm' like?

1. Fast.

2. Entrepreneurial. This firm thinks like she does and is always on the lookout for faster, cheaper ways to get the job done.

3. Out-of-the-box thinkers. This firm doesn't always play by the book because they know how to get around the red tape that can tie up an important project and its crucial funding.

4. Did we say, 'fast?'

Obviously, these two clients are worlds apart in their view of the 'ideal' firm. And the firm that attempts to sell to these two clients using the same pitch, the same project sheets and the same resumes will fail with both of them.

Question #3, Part 1: *What are the reasons that this client might object to hiring you?*

This question is an awkward one and could make you a little uncomfortable. If any of the participants in your meeting have strong egos, they should leave them parked at the door.

As good as you are, there are reasons or perceptions out there that influence clients to steer clear of you. Perhaps it's something straightforward like the fact that your firm is too far from the project site or doesn't have a large enough staff to handle the project. It may be that you are perceived as being high priced or too specialized or not specialized enough.

It may be something more difficult to deal with. Perhaps you have very little experience in this type of project. Maybe you have some recent black marks on your record because a couple of projects came in behind schedule or the quality of your contract documents was questioned by some contractors.

List all the possible objections, real or perceived, the client may have to hiring you on a flip chart sheet and hang it on the wall.

Example
1. Your firm only has 10 staff and the client thinks the project needs more 'horsepower' than that.

2. Your firm is considered an expert in high-tech projects, but this project is focused in a very particular aspect of technology in which you have little experience.

3. Your office is located 150 miles from the project site.

4. Five years ago, one of your principals made a remark in a public meeting that offended the mayor who is now on the Board of Directors of the client's company.

5. Six months ago, you got some bad press because the client was unable to obtain the rezoning they required and blamed you publicly for the failure.

Very often, the selection process is not a question of 'who wins?' Instead it often comes down to, 'who's left standing at the end of an elimination process?' In a competition among virtual equals, your client will be looking for excuses to eliminate contenders. Any of the reasons shown above would be good enough to knock you off the list. If you head into the sales process without knowing about or being prepared to deal with these objections, you might as well not bother at all.

Question #3, Part 2: *What are you going to do about it?*
Now that you've identified all the great reasons that this client should not hire you, what can you do about it? The next step is to take each objection and analyze it by answering the following questions.

1. *Is this objection true or simply a perception on the part of the client?*

    If it is simply a perception, your proposal must reveal the truth.

    Example: The client has heard that several recent projects went over budget and fell behind schedule. You must be prepared to show how the client on those projects significantly expanded the scope of the work.

2. *If the objection is true, how can you show it to be an advantage to the client?*

    Example: The client is concerned about the fact that your firm has only ten staff. You are prepared to explain that a small firm allows you the freedom to think and act like a SWAT team; to move quickly and decisively on any issue. You are also free to go out and hand-pick sub-consultants who are the tops in their field.

3. *If you are unable to show the objection to be an advantage, what will you offer in compensation?*

    Example: The client is concerned that your office is 150 miles from the project. It's hard to show this to be an advantage, so you can explain that you've arranged to lease office space across the street from the project for the duration of the job and staff it with the two key people who will be devoted full time to the project.

4. *If you are unable to show it to be an advantage or offer some compensation, should you risk ignoring this objection and hope the client doesn't notice or have it brought to their attention?*

    This is a very risky option and, by this time you are getting desperate. However, you just might get lucky and have a client who doesn't put much merit in that particular aspect or think to ask about it.

5. *If you ignore the objection and the client does notice, will you immediately be knocked out of the competition?*

    If the issue is indeed a 'killer,' this is a very good time to revisit your Go/No Go decision before you spend any more money on this proposal. Perhaps you have identified an issue that you hadn't noticed before. Better to cut bait and go now, than to spend more money on the sales effort knowing it can't succeed.

Of course, you have to exercise a level of judgment as to whether you actually raise these issues in your business development effort or simply be prepared to address them if they come up. Some issues such as the 150 mile distance from the project site are so obvious that you can't escape them. In these cases, you should be proactive and 'head it off at the pass' by dealing with it before the client has a chance to be concerned. In other issues, such as the one about firm size, it might be best not to mention the point unless the client brings it up. If that happens, you will be prepared with a suitable, confident and convincing answer to their concern.

Detail your responses to the objections on a flip chart sheet and hang it on the wall.

Question #4: *Who will you be competing against on this project?*
This question asks you to list the major competitors you will, or are likely to face in competition for this project. If there are likely to be 20 firms competing on the project, list only the top three or four that are likely to give you serious competition.

Outside the context of any given project, you should stay up to date on new developments within each competitor's firm. If you've kept a regular eye on them you won't have any trouble identifying their strengths and weaknesses.

On a flip chart sheet, and for each competing firm, list:

1. The aspects of the firm that make them so good and likely to beat you

2. The weaknesses that make them fall down and lose projects like this

Be honest in your evaluation of both strengths and weaknesses - they have plenty of both. Your corporate pride makes it far too easy to criticize and say, "they can't do anything right." Obviously they can or they would not be considered competitors.

Question #5: What is the clear added value that you'll bring to this project?
Every one of your competitors will be able to execute the project successfully, on time and within budget. That's junior league stuff. Your client is going to be looking for that special something from the winning firm that will put this project over the top and make the selection decision an easy one. How will you clearly differentiate your firm from all the others?

Will it be?

*   The unique approach you bring to the project?
*   The speed with which you get it done?
*   Your ability to expedite the permitting process?
*   Your low fees?
*   The vastly superior technical knowledge you possess?
*   Your intimate familiarity with the circumstances surrounding this project?

- Your ability to get disparate parties working smoothly together?

- The unexpected, yet wholly convincing alternative you suggest?

- Something else?

Whatever it is, it MUST be something beyond your credentials and your previous experience. Those will get you to the door. The 'something extra' will get you to the win.

On a flip chart sheet, describe how you plan to truly and convincingly set your firm apart from all the others, and hang it on the wall.

Proposal Themes

Your answers to the five brainstorming questions provided you with some remarkable and very valuable information. And you can now use that information to wire this proposal directly to the decision-making center in that client's brain. These answers become vital, client-centered themes that will show the client the proposal was written exclusively for their project. They'll give a consistency and unity to it by weaving these targeted, client-centered themes throughout the entire proposal.

Here's how it works

You clearly described:

1.   What the client wants to buy.
The 'hot buttons' that you identified now become the focus of your sales effort. You've learned that the clients doesn't actually

want to buy a new water distribution system, they want to buy a cold glass of water on a hot summer day. By focusing on their 'end game,' you'll let the client clearly see their own objectives being accomplished through you.

2.   Who the client wants to hire.

The client doesn't want to retain your firm, or anybody else's either. They want to hire that perfect firm that only exists in their imagination. You're going to use the traits of the 'ideal firm' to guide your description of your firm. You're not going to refer to anything about your firm that isn't consistent with that vision and, in doing so, you'll confirm in the client's mind that you are that 'firm of their dreams.'

3.   Why the client might hesitate to hire you.

Armed with this valuable information, you can now tackle and dispel these issues throughout your proposal in order to ease their mind and raise the client's comfort level. And while you might not choose to directly address every one of the possible objections, you will be ready with an answer should they be raised.

4.   The strengths and weaknesses of your competitors.

While you'll never name names, you can certainly use this knowledge to reinforce your position and, perhaps, plant a few 'seeds of doubt' that might get the client to pay extra critical attention to some weaknesses on the part of your competition. You also know the areas to which you'll have to pay extra attention in order to defend against a particular competitor's strength.

5.   The secret sauce that's going to set you apart from all the
     other competitors.
Even with all your credentials lined up in a row so that you are
as shined up and spit-polished as a new Marine on parade day,
you can count on all the competitors to be looking pretty good
too. This 'something extra' will serve as the tie-breaker when it
comes down to choosing between your firm and all the others.

Whenever I work on a proposal I take these five answer sheets
and hang them up in my work space. Then as I'm writing the
cover letter, the project approach statement, the key resumes and
every other proposal section, these answers become a checklist of
issues that I make sure are loud and clear in the proposal.

These answers serve as the themes that occur throughout every
section of the proposal and frequently find their way into the presentation too. You've crawled inside your client's head and seen
how things look from that point of view. Next we'll learn how
to incorporate them into your proposal and presentation efforts.

Step 4: The Art of Persuasion
If you've decided that the project opportunity is worth the time,
effort and money of a response, then you'd better make it a good
one. Proposal writing is not a numbers game—throw enough of
them at the wall and something's bound to stick. No, once you
get past the go/no go filter, you're all in and there's nothing will
do but to win it.

And if you're going to win it, you have two strategy choices:
1.   Play it safe and avoid offending anyone who might give
     your firm a black mark. This is the defensive strategy.

2. Grab their attention by the throat, throw them to the ground with your laser-focused response and take an aggressive approach that leaves them absolutely no choice but to put you at the very top of the short list. This is the offensive tactic.

Since every good coach knows the best defense is a good offense, we're going to use the second strategy to win this particular game.

There is nothing easier in the A/E industry than to come second in a project selection process. It must be easy because so many firms regularly accomplish it!

You never hear, "we came fifth!" All the time it's, "we came second." Or how about, "we came a close second!" (As if that paid more than 'regular' second.) The point is, in this business, you either win or you lose. There is no such thing as second place, just one winner, and a whole string of losers.

I believe very strongly that the riskiest thing a firm can do today is to be normal, predictable and 'safe.' Why is that risky? Because you risk looking exactly like every other firm with which you are competing. And that road leads to commodity pricing.

Right now, stop reading this and go grab some recent proposals you've submitted. I'll wait…

Now that you've got them in your hand, be honest—are they bold, or are they bland and ordinary? Do they command your attention? Do they make you want to read them, or can you instantly tell that it will be an effort to read them?

That prospective new client is looking for a firm that will bring them a unique set of benefits. There are hundreds of firms that can accomplish the work, but only one that has the unique talents and approaches of your firm. The proposal is one of your prime opportunities to strut that singularity.

You're going to make your proposal a clear, proud statement that your firm is not like the rest. Never aim to be 'average' or 'adequate.' Aim to either score a perfect "10," or go down in flames and come dead last with a '0.'

The ultimate goal of your proposal (and, frankly, all your marketing efforts) is to persuade. To persuade that prospect that your firm, above all other competitors, is best suited to take charge of their project.

Persuasion requires that someone change his or her mind. Throughout history people have resorted to a multitude of techniques ranging from love poems to bamboo shoots under the fingernails in the attempt to persuade others. In the marketing realm, however, we've learned that there is a handful of communication tactics that are essential if you have any hope of persuading that prospective client to change her mind and select you.

WIIFM (What's In It For Me?)
Everyone in the world shares the same favorite subject. Ourselves.

And this perennial focus on, 'What's in it for me?' tells the smart salesperson (and business developer, and proposal writer) to focus on the customer, not the service being sold.

Imagine the oh-so-common statement that shows up in virtually every proposal, "Our firm was founded in 1958." (Or whatever your founding year happens to be.) The cynical or preoccupied client would respond simply and rightly, "So what? What is it about the fact that your firm began so long ago that could possibly be of interest or benefit to me?"

The client didn't set out to hire a firm of a particular age. They set out to find a firm that could complete their project on time and within budget, give them extraordinary value for the fees they pay, and ensure a long-lasting, high quality facility. If that firm was founded two weeks ago and has a way to bring those outcomes, the client will hire them.

The fact that your firm has been around for more than half a century is irrelevant. What *is* relevant are the lessons you've learned that will bring them a solution more quickly, the procedures you've developed that will ensure high quality on their project, and the network you've established that will smooth the way for an early completion for their project.

Which brings us to a discussion about:

Features versus Benefits
You know the difference between features and benefits. A feature of the car is that it has 27 airbags. The benefit to the car buyer is that she is much more likely to emerge unharmed after an accident. Bottom line: clients don't buy the features of your firm, they buy benefits that will make their lives easier, less complicated and more successful.

In a recent book I was reading I came across an amazing technique to help keep your marketing efforts focused on client benefits rather than features of your firm. It works like this: Silently add the words, 'which means...' to the end of every statement you make in your proposals and sales presentations. This will remind you to always translate the features of your firm into benefits for the client.

Let's look at some typical examples:

"Our firm was founded in 1958."
...which means that more than half a century of accumulated 'lessons-learned' will eliminate potential mistakes and bring many time- and money-saving ideas to your project.

"Our company has an excellent on-site safety record."
...which means you enjoy lower insurance and overall project costs, peace of mind and happy workers while avoiding negative public relations.

"Our firm has won numerous industry awards."
...which means you share the prestige and recognition and take comfort in our extremely high standard of excellence.

"We have an excellent track record of successful projects."
...which means you will have fewer demands on your time, better decision-making, reduced risk and a much higher likelihood of on-time and on-budget delivery.

"Our firm is the largest in the state."

…which means you enjoy reduced costs through buying power and increased speed through our leverage of suppliers and subcontractors.

"We have the greatest people in the world working here."

…which means that you will enjoy pampered attention, ease of communication, an extended network and easy, timely access to important information.

"Our firm has invested heavily in reliable systems and procedures."

…which means you can trust the information we provide while enjoying reduced risk and the ability to focus your attention on other priorities.

"Our management team is heavily involved in the community."

…which means you benefit from an extended network, the prestige of working with a community leader and direct links to additional opportunities.

I believe you get the point. Your customers and prospects don't care about the features of your company. They only care about the benefits that will accrue to them. So follow your statements with, 'which means…' in order to focus on the benefits and leave the discussion of features to your came-in-second competitor.

Avoiding the Trite Trap
Having read hundreds, if not thousands of design firm proposals, I have concluded that much of what is presented as valuable

content is, in fact, trite and meaningless rubbish.

Sound harsh? To add some science to this otherwise gut-level conclusion, I've developed what I call 'The Trite Test.' It can be applied to any communication, written or verbal, that you send to a prospective client in hopes that he or she will hire you.

Here's how it works:

Since the bottom line of all marketing is differentiation, i.e., "What have you got that the other guy doesn't?" it's reasonable that any marketing statement you make should further distinguish you from them. To apply the Trite Test, ask this question:

"Could I imagine one of my competitors, in an effort to differentiate himself from me, saying the opposite of what I've just said?"

Let's try an example; a tired, worn-out statement used in a proposal cover letter.

"Acme Engineers is pleased to submit this proposal."

Apply the Trite Test and imagine someone writing, *"We're really annoyed at having to prepare and submit this proposal."* Of course not! The fact that you were pleased to submit is self-evident. If you had not been pleased you wouldn't have bothered. So it's a corny statement that adds nothing to your submission.

When you realize that every cover letter of every proposal begins with that same sentence (or a subtle variation of it), it becomes even more clichéd and meaningless. Worse, instead of setting you apart, it only reinforces the perception that your firm is just like everyone else who has submitted.

Here are more hackneyed statements that appear in proposals in one form or another.

"We are uniquely qualified."

While this may be true, the statement by itself proves nothing. Instead of using this stale and ever-present assertion, get specific and cite examples of your unique qualifications: *"Our unique scheduling process will ensure the smooth operation of the rest of your facility during construction."*

"Our firm has been in business for XX years."

If a firm is more than 25 years old, all the old guys are either retired or dead and no one is getting the benefit of their experience. Besides, experience gained on projects more than 15 years old is irrelevant today. The client did not set out to hire a firm with a specific number of years' experience. They want a firm that can solve today's problem regardless of how long it's been in business. Don't talk about years of experience, talk about the lessons you've learned, captured and shared. Relate a case study of a lesson-learned that was applied to another project and how that client benefited. The statement that your firm has been in business 100 years could easily be interpreted to mean that it's just old and tired!

"We will meet your schedule and budget."

Imagine going to buy a new car and having the salesman tell you that you should buy this car because "it will start every morning!" Reliability like that became available long ago and we've moved on to much higher expectations. Clients today fully expect that you will meet schedule and budget – that's merely the ante to the game. Instead, show how you're going to go above and beyond the minimum requirement.

"We will exceed your expectations."

'Nuf said.

Trite clichés do nothing to inspire a client to prefer your firm over another. Instead, they strongly reinforce the impression that yours is just like all the others. Ask a trusted client if you can borrow some old proposals they've received from other firms. Review them and see for yourself just how much they sound like yours. Then purge all the tired, commonplace and unoriginal statements from your marketing and sales efforts so you can truly stand apart from the crowd.

An Accessible Writing Style

David Ogilvy, considered by some to be the father of modern advertising, was responsible for a revolution in how companies communicated with their customers through their marketing.

"I don't know the rules of grammar. . . . If you're trying to persuade people to do something, or buy something, it seems to me you should use their language, the language they use every day, the language in which they think. We try to write in the vernacular.

David Ogilvy

One of the most effective persuasion techniques is to make the content of your proposal easily accessible and understood. Too many technical professionals have been trained in technical writing and use that style in their proposals.

Sure, technical writing may be accurate, but it's hang-me-now-please boring to read. You want to generate excitement and enthusiasm in your reader and that doesn't happen from perusing something that reads like a specification.

Instead, try writing in a more comfortable, easy-going style. One of the tests you can use to check your writing is to read a passage that you've written out loud to yourself. Then ask, "Does this sound like me talking?" If it sounds a little (or a lot!) too stiff and formal, rewrite it and relax your writing style.

If you've spent your entire career writing technical reports, this might, at first, seem a little too casual for you. But relaxing your writing style makes it so much easier for your clients to understand and retain your message. And isn't that an important step in persuasion?

Left Brain, Right Brain

Every time I make it safely to the far side of a bridge and every time I'm enjoying the view from the 50th floor, I say a silent one in thanks for all the wonderful engineers and architects in the world and their fabulous, left-brained thinking. I have enormous admiration and appreciation for the logic, the rationale, and the discipline required to be a design professional.

But when it comes to persuading a client to buy your services, a larger dose of right brain would go a long way.

Architects and engineers think, and have been trained to communicate in ways that are logical, factual and rational. A well-written technical paper, for example, lets the reader evaluate the facts and not be influenced by hype, opinion or emotion. But when these communication techniques are used in proposals and marketing materials you risk boring and even alienating all the non-technical types who might be making important decisions about hiring you. Not everybody thinks like you.

In fact, the population has a broad spectrum of communication preferences. Cognitive Psychology is an entire science devoted to studying how people take in information, process it, and reach decisions. And the non-technical people of the world communicate and understand best, not through the sorting of facts and data, but through stories, allegory, examples and — yes — emotion.

It's a bit of an over-simplification, but it's quite safe to say that communication preferences are linked to the four basic personality types:

- The person who values intellect needs to understand your logic.

- The person who values feelings needs to perceive your motives.

- The person who values stability needs to know it has been tested.

- The person who values courage needs to hear you speak of action.

The best writers, speakers and presenters speak to each of these four people every time they attempt to persuade.

Putting something into your proposal or presentation for each of them broadens your conversation and makes it easier for each individual to positively connect with you. People don't all communicate in the same way. Learn to speak to all four preferences and your voice will carry rich, persuasive harmony.

You're selling to humans, not machines
Now, let's get back to that important question:

Why should a client hire <u>you</u>?

They will hire you because you realize that your client is a human being, not a computer or a spreadsheet. If you were trying to sell your services to a computer, you would analyze your capabilities on a spreadsheet and the winning firm would quickly become obvious.

Human beings, however, respond only marginally to spreadsheets and more positively to arguments that are equal parts enthusiasm, energy, excitement and, yes, logic.

In order to persuade successfully, start by learning how the 'persuadee' thinks. Crawl inside their heads, find out what's important to them and identify the benefits they're seeking. Once you understand the 'view' from your client's side of the desk, tell them how the direct benefits they'll enjoy while working with you will be the answer to their every prayer. And while you're at it, leave the trite statements to your competition.

7.2 WRITING THE PROPOSAL

Proposal Contents

Your proposal is not just a technical document conveying data. It has to persuade, assure, convince, comfort, and win over a client who is about to put a great deal of money and trust in your hands. A proposal is not only about qualifications. It's a personal message.

To be sure, clients aren't much help when it comes to rethinking how we write and structure our proposals. They've been stuck in the same ruts, for just as long as we have. The RFPs they send out reinforce our old habits of submitting cold, lifeless data in list after list that simply confirm how much we look just like our competitors.

Here is an excerpt from an actual RFP issued by a municipal client looking to retain design services. It describes what the City would like to see in the proposal responses.

The proposal shall include:

1. *Size and make-up of the firm.*

2. *Names and resumes of personnel to be assigned to the project.*

3. *A list of related projects and references.*

4. *A list of other disciplines that would be included in the proposal.*

5. *Previous experience with similar projects.*

6. *Proven ability to adhere to schedules and budgets, within particular emphasis on design consulting.*

7. *A description of the methodology and procedures to be used for the total scope of this project. (i.e., concept phase, design phase, public input phases).*

8.   *Fees disbursement and hourly charge-out rates for the concept design phase.*

Taken at face value, this becomes a handy checklist that can be given to a Marketing Coordinator, assembled and submitted to the client for review. It would be filled with boilerplate and generic answers that are copied and pasted from the answers given in previous proposals to other clients.

But this would entirely miss the point!

Instead of taking a checklist approach to your proposal, you need to crawl inside the client's head and discover what it is they're actually looking for. Instead of taking a checklist approach, read the list above again and realize that what the client really meant to say was:

The proposal shall include:

Sufficient information, presented in a concise, easy-to-access and persuasive manner that will conclusively show the selection committee why yours is the only firm on the face of this planet that should even be considered for this project.

If the RFP were written in that way, you might think twice about the mind-numbing lists that make up the bulk of your submissions.

Contrary to commonly held beliefs, and in order to 'hot wire' your firm to your client's brain, you must think in terms of there being only three sections in a good proposal:

1. First Impressions – in which you grab the client's attention and draw her into an interesting and engaging document.

2. What We're Going To Do For You – in which you relate the services you're about to provide and how the client's world will be so much better for having worked with you.

3. Who We Are – in which you demonstrate that your firm is an exact match with that imaginary firm they'd love to hire, if only it existed.

Of course you can't think of these three categories as you would normal sections separated by tabbed dividers. Instead, think of them as three critical messages that have to be delivered to your client—sometimes subliminally.

These three sections will be intermingled through the proposal because they client will likely have specified the tabbed sections you're to include. As you write, recast the standard, traditional proposal sections into this new context. At all times, imagine yourself as the client, having to review and evaluate the proposal. Is your writing style interesting and engaging? Is your fit for this project obvious? Do the photos and illustrations you've chosen complement the message and add understanding and clarity?

Clients in this business are as bad at writing RFPs as we are at writing proposals. And they use the same techniques – 'Save As,' and cut-and-paste. When you're preparing your next submittal, don't ignore the client's instructions, but go beyond the checklist and give them a proposal response that blows their socks off.

1. The 'First Impressions' Section

Scary story # 1:
Some years ago I was facilitating a proposal writing workshop with about 20 CEOs from a **variety** of design firms. I had a stack of proposals and I asked the group to think of themselves as a client selection panel. Their job was to review the proposals and reduce the large pile to two smaller ones: the short list and the rejects.

We passed out the proposals and these high-ranking executives dove into them. What these CEOs did not know was that I was timing how long they took to make that initial decision about 'Pile A' or 'Pile B.'

Here's the scary part: The average time spent with each proposal before making that initial, crucial decision was 18 seconds. 18 seconds! It takes longer than that to brush your teeth! And yet these executives were willing to make important decisions based on the information they could assimilate in that incredibly short time.

Scary story # 2:
More recently I had occasion to be at the NAVFAC (Naval Facilities Command) in Norfolk, VA where I was meeting with one of the Navy's Contracting Officers. She related how, in response to an RFP, she had received 40 proposals. Lacking the time to review them all she instructed her assistant to line all the proposals up, leaning on the ledge below the white boards in the conference room. She then proceeded to walk into the room and, from a distance of 10 feet, select the 12 proposals she would review in detail.

All that incredibly detailed information over which you agonized and slaved was never even seen. Yes, we do judge books by their covers.

Have you ever thought about how your client actually reviews your proposal? By this I mean the physical process of looking at it for the first time? It goes like this: if your client is right handed, she holds the proposal in her right hand and flips through it with her left thumb, starting from the back and moving to the front.

As she does this she's observing how the pages are laid out, the kind of paper that it's printed on and any interesting graphics that might be included. Then she flips to the front and finds the cover letter. She begins to scan the letter and if the 18-second clock expires and she's still not seen anything that she thinks deserves further consideration, your proposal goes into the reject pile.

So what we need to do is to take that First Impressions section, and learn to maximize the communication of information in that short period of time. What we have to do is learn how to communicate key information very, very quickly. Because unless we learn how to do that all that good stuff that's there in the middle of page 12 will never be seen.

The 'First Impressions' section is intended to make an instant and significant impact and consists of:

- The outside cover
- The binding you've used

- The title you've given the document
- The page design, paper, and fonts you've used
- The cover letter you've written

Let's talk about each of these.

The Outside Cover

The cover of your proposal is like the packaging a retailer uses to market their products. Think about the three different shopping bags you get shopping at Wal-Mart, Macy's, and Saks Fifth Avenue. Each bag tells a very different story about the store, the quality of the products it sells, and the type of customer it hopes to attract.

You never hear Saks' customers complaining about the cost of the fancy shopping bag or the salary of the uniformed doorman as they pull up on Rodeo Drive in Beverly Hills. But they know perfectly well those costs are added to the price of the products they buy. Nor do you hear Wal-Mart customers asking to have a doorman or more up-scale store fixtures. They also know these costs would add to the overhead of the store and passed on to them.

Your job will be to choose the packaging that's appropriate for the project at hand. Each one might be different—fancy enough for the sophisticated, high-end client, and plain enough for the meat-and-potatoes folks. Fortunately, you have plenty of options.

Attractive Cover Images

It's a good idea to have an attractive and eye-catching photographic image on the cover of your proposal. It can convey a sense of the value you're going to bring to the project and add to that all-important first impression.

Many firms have a photo on the cover of their proposals, but the choices that are made are pretty questionable. There is nothing attractive or engaging about a photo of a piece of PVC pipe lying in the bottom of a muddy trench. There's a reason we end up burying this stuff—it's not nice to look at!

Instead of the predictable photos of completed projects, use lifestyle photos that show the end users enjoying the benefits of your work. We put the pipe there for the benefit it brings: Clean water from a tap. So let's have a photo of a cute three-year old enjoying a glass of cold water on a hot summer day.

Instead of a shot of the waste treatment plant, how about a little boy having his Saturday night bath. Instead of an empty intersection and traffic signals, why not pedestrians and cyclists safely crossing through traffic? Instead of a photo of the outside of a shopping center, taken early Sunday morning when there's no one around, use an image of bustling shoppers and busy stores.

I know there are rules about signing waivers for people in photos, but get the staff from your office or hire your cousin to sit on the bench or have the photo taken so the faces are moving and blurred. Your project was designed to accommodate humans— let's see a few populating it!

If you don't have the right photo, go online to some of the great stock photo services you can find online. Professional-quality digital photos are available for just a few bucks. Make sure you select 'Royalty Free' and purchase the image at a resolution that is high enough to be clear and sharp on your cover.

An Eye-Catching Title

The titles of most proposals are as dull as grey paint. Why not jazz things up a little? A good title is like a headline in a newspaper article, it grabs your attention and hints at what you can expect to discover.

If schedule is going to be a big deal on your project, refer to on-time delivery in the title. If there is a significant technical challenge on the project, work your solution into the title and splash it on the cover. Here are some examples based on an actual RFP for A/E services for a Federal correctional facility. (The actual names have been changed.) The RFP from the client was titled:

Request for Proposal for Architect/Engineering Services

Federal Correctional Facilities

Podunk County, GA

SOL RFP X00-1234

Federal Bureau of Prisons

The predictable, traditional reaction would be to title the proposal:

Response to Request for Proposal for Architect/Engineering Services

Federal Correctional Facilities

Podunk County, GA

SOL RFP X00-1234

Federal Bureau of Prisons

Not only is this boring and unimaginative, it fails to tell the client anything they don't already know. It doesn't reflect any of the unique aspects of your firm and it doesn't respond to any of the issues that the project may face. Lastly, it fails to differentiate you from any competitor because you can guarantee they will all use the same title. Surely we can do better than this.

Using the 'headline' idea, if a major hot button on the project is schedule, why not try:

Georgia Prison Locked Up in 28 Months

If the big challenge is cost control you could use:

Under Lock, Key, and Budget in Georgia

Look to the type of project to give you ideas about an innovative title:

A renovation project for a corporate client:

Updating Your Investment in the Phoenix Building

A road reconstruction for a municipality:

Keeping the Traffic Flowing at Maple and Elm Streets

A student housing center:

Housing Our Future Leaders at Jefferson College

You can also reference the RFP and your firm identification on the cover if you want, although it's not always necessary. But make the title and the image something that will set you apart from everyone else and intrigue and delight the reader. Give some hint about the contents of your proposal and help your client to pay attention.

Bindings

Choosing an attractive and appropriate binding system for your proposal tells the client that you care enough to think about packaging it in something other than the same old predictable thing. There are plenty of options available, so why not get creative?

Plastic Comb

Used for 99.9% of all proposals. It looks cheap and is cheap. It's also old. While some firms 'customize' the binding by having their name printed on the spine, it doesn't remove the low rent image.

Plastic Spiral

Still low end, but a step up from comb binding.

Metal Wire

Metal wire binding is inexpensive but more classy than plastic.

3-Ring Binder

Binders can look very smart, especially the type with a clear plastic cover. This allows you to create a custom cover page that includes your eye-catching images and headline title.

Hard Covers

There are many binding systems available today that make it easy and inexpensive to put together professional-looking "books" quickly and at low cost.

Totally Customized

I've seen proposal covers that had been created from tree bark, sewn by hand, welded from metal, crafted from cork board and a whole host of other, incredibly creative options. In each case, the cover and binding was an imaginative and customized response to that particular client's needs and situation. Get creative!

I once saw a proposal submitted to a developer in Chicago by a design/build team of architects and contractors. The project was a very high-end condominium project—the sort for which you pay $3 million for a one-bedroom unit. The proposal document was hardbound in black leather with gold leaf lettering on the front cover! It even smelled rich! Any client, picking up that document would immediately know that the design/build team had completely understood the nature of the project.

Don't get me wrong. The Public Works Director reviewing your proposal to conduct smoke tests on his sanitary sewer system would not appreciate the gesture!

The point is that you have choices. Make the appropriate choice based on what you know of the client and the project from your research, your brainstorming and your game plan.

An Attractive Page Design

The information you need to convey to your client can be obscured, if not completely hidden by a poorly designed page. It is a mistake to assume that since the words are on the page, the reader will find, read, and understand them. A well-designed page will aid dramatically in prioritizing and communicating the information it holds.

There are a few simple rules that will make you a master page designer.

1.   Find or prepare a page design that is attractive, simple and effective and stick with it. Don't continually mess around with alternative page layouts. It wastes your time and doesn't substantially improve your proposals.

2.   Separate the discrete pieces of information in your proposal into separate blocks of text on the page. Allow enough space between distinct thoughts to allow the readers eyes to rest and assimilate what you've just said. If the thought is important enough, start a new page with a new heading.

3.   Use an invisible grid to organize your layout so each page looks similar. If all the elements on each page (titles, graphics, text, pictures) conform to the grid you will have achieved a uniform, consistent look throughout the entire proposal. Let's look at an example of how this works.

If you are stuck for ideas, look in books and magazines and copy the layouts of the pages you find attractive. Measure the margins and the spaces between columns of text and duplicate it in your proposal. If you find it appealing, your clients will likely do so as well.

Better yet, retain the services of a professional graphic designer to prepare a proposal template for you. Have them design the location of text and picture blocks, suggest white space areas and choose fonts and color schemes. Then STICK TO IT. Don't try to tweak it. Remember: you're a professional engineer or architect. You don't expect people to start 'tweaking' your bridge or building designs. You know what you're doing and you expect your clients to trust you. So does the graphic designer.

A Nice Piece of Paper
Your choices in paper stock range all the way from hand made, recycled sheets with chunks of wood floating around in it, to high gloss, high tech, metallic paper. There are also pre-printed sheets that can run through your laser printer for a custom look at low cost.

These papers are also easy to find and obtain. There are numerous mail order paper companies who will send you five or five thousand sheets, with matching covers, envelopes, and note cards, depending on what you want. You no longer have any excuse for submitting a boring document on 20 pound, white bond paper.

However, just because these papers are available, it does not mean you should automatically use them. Just as you will choose a cover and binding appropriate to the project and the client, you should choose paper stock that sends the same, consistent message.

If the project is high class and elegant, select something refined. If it's an environmental job, use recycled paper. If the culture of the organization you are proposing to is creative and upbeat, select a paper stock that reinforces that message.

There are even times when the best choice is your own office stationery. Just don't assume that to be the case for every proposal.

Well Chosen Fonts

Today there are thousands of fonts to choose from and the selection can be overwhelming to the untrained eye. Here's an easy rule to remember: <u>Most</u> of the fonts that came loaded on your computer should <u>never</u> be used in your proposals because they are too 'cute' or unusual.

There are two major font groups—Serif and Sans Serif. Serif refers to any font in which the letters have the small tags at their ends. It should almost always be used for blocks of text because that little tag actually allows the eye to move smoothly from one letter and word to the next. Sans Serif refers to those fonts that don't have the tags. They can provide a more 'contemporary' look but make reading blocks of text more difficult. They should be reserved for headings and titles.

Serif fonts which you should commonly use include:

Times
Palatino
Garamond

Sans serif fonts that are useful include:

Helvetica
Geneva
Ariel

Keep your selection of fonts to a minimum to avoid a busy look to your page.

Your proposal can achieve all the highlighting and emphasis necessary by choosing one serif and one sans serif font and varying size, emphasis, and capitalization.

ALL CAPITALS
SMALL CAPITALS
Bold
Italic

With the technology we have available, font selection is far too easy and the results are often garish. It will be a good return on your investment to engage a professional graphic designer to suggest some font families that will make your proposals elegant and eye-pleasing.

A Unique Cover Letter
Your cover letter can significantly influence your client's initial reaction to your proposal. It's one of the first items the client reads in the crucial early seconds of their review and it plays an important role in forming their first impressions.

Most firms treat it as a simple transmittal letter and fill it with trite, meaningless statements such as "we are pleased to submit this proposal," or "we are uniquely qualified," and "if you have any questions, please call." These sentences appear in virtually every proposal and only reinforce the client's impression that all firms are the same. In contrast, your objective should be to do everything possible to underscore the differences between you and everyone else.

Your cover letter ought to be so powerful that your client could make up his or her mind by reading it alone. It needs to be comprehensive enough to put you on the short list but short enough to be quickly scanned and understood.

Here's how to do it. Let's say you are proposing design services for a new medical center and your brainstorming session has resulted in the following issues:

Hot Buttons
- Completing the project within 18 months
- Maintaining positive community relations
- Maintaining ongoing operations during construction
- Control over a very tight budget

Ideal Firm
- Located within 20 minutes of the project
- Willing to accept input of Board of Directors and doctors
- Full service firm with all in-house disciplines
- Project manager who has extensive medical center experience

Objections to your firm

- Located 100 miles away from the project   (true)

- Lacks in-house engineering staff   (true)

- Project manager has little   (false)
  medical center experience

- Not the firm we've always worked with   (true)

Competition

Acme Architects	+ high quality contract documents - poor reputation for budget control
Ace Architects	+ strong project management - reputation for poor client relations
Long & Short A/E	+ worked with client before - high priced

Using these hot buttons as an outline, your cover letter can address the project and the client's specific issues like this:

Dr. John Smith
Western Medical Center
123 State Street
Yourtown, ST 12345

Re: Strong staff and community relations on the project

Dear Dr. Smith,

The Western Medical Center's new Pediatric project provides a wonderful opportunity for the hospital to reinforce its strong community ties and staff relationships. By emphasizing the input of your Board and doctors, we fully expect that your aggressive 18-month schedule can be met within budget.

Smith and Jones has been studying this project extensively and has developed a unique scheduling process that will ensure the smooth operation of the rest of your facility during construction. To make the process as smooth as possible we have already mapped out a schedule of community information meetings to invite comments from the surrounding neighborhood.

In addition, you can look forward to:

- *A thoughtful and coordinated process for input by Board and staff members (see page 12)*

- *A project manager with a remarkable talent for smooth community relations (page 8)*

- *A peaceful night's sleep with the knowledge that budget is well under control (see page 4)*

Although you have not had the opportunity to work with Smith and Jones previously, many of your peers have found the experience economical, efficient, professional, and downright pleasant! We invite you to review their comments that can be found throughout this proposal. In addition, working with Smith & Jones on this project will give you the opportunity to compare the levels of service, responsiveness, quality, and economy you have received from other firms.

I will contact you during the next week to clarify any questions you may have regarding our approach to the project. In the meantime, we are continuing to review the specifics of this project and prepare for kickoff.

Yours frugally,
Smith and Jones, Inc.
John J. Jones

PS We are looking forward to demonstrating our unique cost control process at the interview.

This entire letter was built around the important client issues and avoids those 'mom-and-apple-pie' statements used by everyone else.

You'll also notice some other techniques:

- Giving each bullet point a page reference allows a reader intrigued by that issue to go straight to the relevant page.

- Using the signatory line to touch another hot button. It doesn't always have to be 'Yours Truly.'

- The "PS" is guaranteed to be read. Even if they skim your letter, they will always stop and read it. Use it to hit another hot button.

It's not surprising that the majority of selection committee participants admit they have significantly made up their minds shortly after picking up a proposal. It's in your best interest to make the most of this opportunity by making a memorable first impression.

2.   The 'What We're Going To Do For You' Section

Imagine this bizarre scenario:

You are about to take the major step of constructing a new home. You and your spouse are interviewing builders and hoping to select one that will create your dream home. Each builder takes you on a wonderful tour of projects they have done for other people, they provide you with long lists of homes they have built and describe in detail how happy each of their previous customers is with their new home.

But when you ask about the home they will build for you, they never seem to come up with anything better than generic statements about how it will be a 'quality home' made with 'the best materials.' It's unlikely that you'd be willing to hire any of these builders because they either refuse or are unable to see the world from your point of view and get specific about the solution that <u>you</u> are seeking.

This is the situation in which many clients of design professionals find themselves. When it comes right down to it, a client doesn't much care what you've done for someone else. They are first and foremost concerned with what you're going to do for them. Your past experience and credentials are only important because they *suggest* what you are likely to do now.

Clients are happy to hear about your experience but, sooner or later, they want you to get specific about what you can do for them. The 'What We're Going To Do For You' section of your proposal gives your client a clear idea of exactly what they are buying.

Let's be clear—there is never a tabbed section in your proposal titled, "What We'll Do For You." I'm simply using that heading to refer to all the information that you'll include in your proposal that tells the client what they're going to get, how you plan to deliver it and how the experience of working with you will differ from that of working with any other firm.

There are often (although not always) four major components in this section:

1.   A Statement of Understanding
2.   The Scope of Work
3.   Your Approach to the Project
4.   A Definition of the Client's Responsibilities

Statement of Understanding

This is your opportunity to set your firm apart from the crowd by demonstrating your knowledge of the client's needs and expectations. To do this successfully, you've got to show the real insight you've gained into the situation through your research and brainstorming. It's no good to simply repeat the statements that were made in the RFP.

Here's a good example:

An actual RFP read, in part:

> *The City intends to commission the services of a qualified A/E firm to develop concept plans for the overall design of a new aquatic center and recreation facility to be placed before the public at a referendum in November.*

The predictable response in a Statement of Understanding would be to write something like:

> *Smith and Jones understands that the City requires a qualified A/E firm to develop concept plans for the overall design of a new aquatic center and recreation facility. In addition, these plans will be used to present to the public in a referendum in November.*

As uninspiring as this is, I've seen far too many proposals with statements that are equally unimaginative.

Your job is to show the client that you <u>truly</u> understand the challenge they face and that your services will actually provide a solution to their problem. Perhaps your response could sound more like this:

> *At Smith and Jones we have spent considerable time investigating the details and circumstances surrounding the new aquatic center and recreation facility. With the level of public support for this project currently at about 50/50 we know that the City will not only need an attractive and functional design, you will require a compelling and enthusiastic presentation at the public meeting prior to the referendum in November. We intend to work not only with your staff, but with your Council members as well in order to make the design work together with public opinion so this project can be a success.*

A statement like this demonstrates that you have insight behind the mere checklist of things to be done. You are willing to become an active team member who not only provides design and technical expertise, but contributes to the solution of the 'big picture.'

Whenever you are writing a Statement of Understanding you should avoid generic statements that are applicable in any situation - it will come off sounding like boilerplate. A statement such as:

We understand this project must meet your program requirements while maintaining both schedule and budget.

is trite, obvious and absolutely meaningless. Every project has this requirement. Show that you've done your homework by taking the client's issues and adding value, interpretation and insight in a short, concise statement.

Scope of Work

Your statement of scope needs to be a specific listing of what the client can expect to receive in exchange for their money and their trust in you.

One of the most effective ways of delineating your services is through a *Work Breakdown Structure*. A WBS allows you to organize a large complex undertaking such as a project and break it down into logical work packages. It also lends itself well to diagram form, simplifying your task of communicating a complex scope.

A Work Breakdown Structure breaks the overall project into its component parts, each of which can be seen as a mini project on its own. A simple diagram explains the concept.

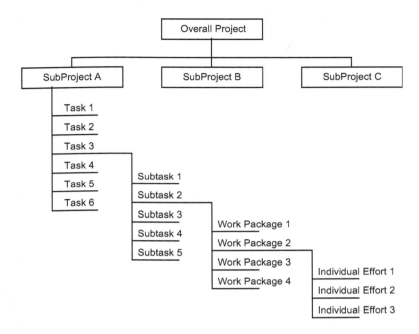

The beauty of the Work Breakdown Structure is not only its ability to communicate scope to a client, it helps you identify the tasks that will be necessary to complete a project. By beginning with a simplistic description of the overall project and working systematically through the job, you can develop a very complete listing of the tasks involved.

The work breakdown structure is also a wonderful aid for discussions with your client. It clearly identifies all the tasks that are necessary for completion of the project. Should the client wish to cut costs, they can easily see the implications of removing one task or another.

It's also useful in discussions regarding who will be responsible for which tasks. By laying them out in the WBS, you can conveniently assign responsibility to yourself, a subconsultant or the client. This can form the basis of project planning discussions and contract negotiations.

Whether or not you use a Work Breakdown Structure, your Scope of Work should essentially be a series of five lists. You need to define:

1.   What are the services to be included?
     This is done best with a detailed listing or the Work Breakdown Structure.

2.   What are the services that are specifically excluded?
     Those items that are not included should be spelled out in detail. For example:

     The study will make use of available data, visual observations and interviews with end users. It will not include extensive research into the detailed system parameters, load calculations or drawing updates.

3.   What are the services that are optionally available?
     Services or approaches that are outside the Scope of Work need to be identified and offered to the client as choices.

     At your discretion, the City may choose for us to pursue an alternate design approach, which our visual inspection of the project site has identified. We feel this alternate design approach can provide significant savings in long term operating costs but could increase initial construction costs by as much as five percent.

4.   What are the services that will be provided at no charge?
     Everybody likes 'free' stuff. So why not provide your client

with 'free' services? Before you get up in arms about the ethics of providing free professional services, let's make sure we understand the definition of 'free.'

'Free' means the charge is not represented as a line item on your bill.

The mints on the pillow at the Ritz Carlton are 'free.' The first three years of scheduled maintenance on your new car are also 'free.' What might you include as 'free' when providing your services? How about:

The following services will be provided at no charge:

- *The first five client-initiated change orders*
- *Rendered 3D model for use by your Marketing Department*
- *Representation at two public meetings*
- *Post completion inspection at six months after start-up*

By offering these small items at 'no charge,' you increase the perceived value of the overall service you provide.

5. The set of deliverables the client can expect upon completion. This should be in the form of a detailed list to protect you down the road from assumptions. For example:

The deliverables from this project will be:

1. *Written project plan presented at the project kickoff meeting.*
2. *Development and maintenance of a project schedule.*
3. *A written description of the construction guidelines compatible with the technology to be installed.*
4. *Drawings of cable and terminal installations.*

5. *Requirements for installation of cable and terminals.*
6. *Written cable and terminal testing requirements.*
7. *Detailed cable and terminal specifications.*
8. *RFP and addenda for supply of cable and terminals.*
9. *Recommendation of cable and terminal contractor.*
10. *Written requirements for documentation of cable and terminal installation including cable records, testing and as-built drawings.*

Project Approach

Unlike the Scope of Services that details *what* you are going to do, the Project Approach defines *how* you intend to go about the project. In discussions with your client, this is a wonderful opportunity to differentiate your firm from another with added value.

How will you tackle this project differently than you handled the last one? What's different about the project and your firm that requires a different and presumably better approach? What is it about this client and their situation that calls for changes or supplements to previous approaches?

Keep in mind that at all times you are attempting to differentiate yourself from your competitors. And trust me, if you tell your client that their project is exactly the same as all the others you've done, it might be the truth but it's not going to go over well.

There are often project areas where a unique approach may be critical. Examples include:

1. Should you invite your client to become involved in the design, perhaps through a charette or public input process?

2.   Is there a proprietary process owned by you or the client that should be used? One construction company has developed and trade-marked a process by which they calculate the total cost of facility ownership under various value-engineering scenarios.

3.   Could an alternative approach to project sequencing ease the ability to maintain ongoing operations through the construction process?

There are many areas where your unique approach can provide a competitive edge and an advantage on the project:

- Scheduling
- Subcontracting and Subconsulting
- Quality Control and Quality Assurance
- Public input
- Permitting
- Value engineering
- Designer-Contractor relations

Here is an example of an approach statement regarding the environmental permitting process. Notice how the statements are very specific. The client reading this can envision this process unfolding on their project. At the same time, they are getting the sense that this team has been down this road before.

There are two key elements to smooth and efficient environmental permitting. First, have a good project! If the project is well designed, makes a real attempt to minimize environmental impact (or, better yet, affects a positive change), and is within all of the agency's rules and guidelines, then there are very few roadblocks that can delay or derail the review process. Second, good communication with the regulatory staff allows them to become familiar with the project before they actually review it, highlights the benefits of the project, minimizes potential confusion and provides the staff with a comfort level about the integrity of the design team and, by extension, the design itself.

We would accomplish these two important goals by first, integrating the environmental permitting team into the design effort so that they can be providing feedback and suggestions which will keep the design within regulatory restrictions and add elements that will help regulators see the overall environmental benefits of the project. We would also keep in constant communication with regulatory staff to ensure that they are up-to-date with their understanding of the project and that they have everything they need to efficiently review the project.

Here is another example of a well-structured approach statement. As you can see, this narrative also helps define the limits of the scope of work.

Approach to the Work

This is how we intend to approach the Long Island Road Interpretive Report. Of course, all work will conform with the guidelines set out by the State Historical Society and to the Secretary of the Interior's Standards for Identification and Evaluation of historic properties.

1. Project Coordination

Our architectural history staff will meet with the State DOT to discuss the project schedule and objectives. We'll be looking for their

*approval of the schedule and proposed activities before any work gets
under way. We will also meet with the archeological staff of the Valley
Archaeology Center to coordinate the efforts on this project.*

2 . Background Research
*We will research the relevant historic and architecture contexts for
the communities and resources along the Long Island Road. Sufficient
information will be gathered to develop historic themes within the project area. Collections that will be consulted include local and county
histories, historic photographs, newspapers and city directories; archi-
val holdings of the State Historical Society's Historic Preservation
Division; collections of local historical societies and organizations and
collections of local public libraries within the project area.*

3 . Two Public Meetings
*Two initial meetings will be held to introduce the project, the Project
Manager and the team to the public. A member of the archeological
staff will attend one of these two meetings. We will use visual displays
to illustrate the goals of the project for the interested citizens. Public
questions and comments will be addressed.*

Hero Stories
Your Project Approach section can also benefit from 'hero stories' in which you have used a unique method with positive
results. Success stories are an enormously effective tool in persuading a client to choose your firm.

This anecdote gave the client a real insight into the firm's
approach and helped a large construction company win a pres-
tigious project in downtown Washington, DC.

When we renovated six floors of the historic bank facility on Pennsylvania Avenue, the greatest challenge was to renovate the first floor banking hall while maintaining full banking services. With careful staging, night shifts for the dirty work and continuous clean-up operations such as we intend to use on your project, we kept every customer clean, protected and happy as we reworked the marble teller counters to their original, 1920 configuration.

Remember that it's your job is to persuade your client to change his or her mind. Hero stories and detailed descriptions of the approach you intend to take allow the client to mentally visualize your firm doing the work. They can begin to picture you running the meetings, negotiating with the Public Works Department and walking the site with the contractor. The more stories you tell and the more specific you are, the clearer that picture becomes.

By painting a mental picture of you actually working on their project you come a long way towards persuading them to hire you and not someone else.

Defining the Client's Responsibilities
Something that is often overlooked in the proposal process is to clearly define the roles of each player. Since you won't be able to do the work effectively without input and contribution from the client, your project approach statements should also spell out what you need and expect from them. Here's an example that shows how you can detail this in your proposal.

Acme Corporation's Responsibilities

We all want this project to flow as smoothly and efficiently as possible. To accomplish that, Acme must be an active participant in the process. Among your major responsibilities will be:

1. *Provide a single project coordinator who is dedicated to the successful completion of this job.*

2. *Provide complete and accurate documentation of the existing systems and services in the facility.*

3. *Make timely decisions consistent with the schedule we have prepared to allow our work and the work of other consultants and contractors to stay on schedule.*

4. *Keep us informed of any physical, organizational or other changes during the course of the project that might influence the outcome of the project. In short, this project must be a collaborative effort between the Acme Corporation and Smith and Jones Engineers.*

Statements like this make it clear that you have not only thought the project through and identified areas where glitches may occur, you have also taken a leadership position in coordinating the effort that will be needed. This builds confidence on the part of a client who is looking for a consultant that will come in, take charge, and make the problem go away.

Most proposals spend most of their space talking about the firm's experience and other people's projects. While this is important, it's not nearly as important as what you're going to do for your client on THIS project. The 'What We'll Do For You' section is your opportunity to really stand out from the crowd and get your client drooling over the idea of working with you.

3. The 'Who We Are' Section

Let's go back to the beginning of our discussion about proposals and review the list of requirements that the client included in their RFP.

THE PROPOSAL SHALL INCLUDE

1. *Size and make-up of the firm.*

2. *Names and resumes of personnel to be assigned to the project.*

3. *A list of related projects and references.*

4. *A list of other disciplines that would be included in the proposal.*

5. *Previous experience with similar projects.*

6. *Proven ability to adhere to schedules and budgets, within particular emphasis on design consulting.*

7. *A description of the methodology and procedures to be used for the total scope of this project. (i.e., concept phase, design phase, public input phases).*

8. *Fees disbursement and hourly charge-out rates for the concept design phase.*

Of the eight items on the list, five are inquiring about your firm, your capabilities and the team you intend to use.

In order to be comfortable in their decision, your client must develop a level of trust in your ability to deliver what you promise. We discussed this at length in Chapters 3 and 4. Recall that, since you're not selling cars that can be taken for a test drive and objectively compared, the client has no option but to look at your history and past performance as an indicator of how you're likely to perform on their project.

The 'Who We Are' section is designed to reduce or eliminate the client's sense of risk when hiring you by establishing and reinforcing your capability to execute the project at hand.

Relevant Experience

In my brief moments of cynicism, I find myself referring to the proposal process for most projects as 'The Battle of the Lists.' Proposals are introduced by a low-impact cover letter indicating that the firm has lots of relevant experience. The proposal then goes on to list the projects the firm has done. These projects are shown in numerous areas including resumes, approach statements, experience and other places too. The lists carefully enumerate all the projects that the firm has done, giving the project name, the client, the completion date and, usually, the construction cost.

Unfortunately however, these lists do little or nothing to show the value that you brought to a client's project or the value that you will bring to this one. Take, for example, the following list of housing projects that was pulled from a typical proposal. (The project names have been changed.)

Golden Age Retirement Village
> *101 Elderly units and community building*
> *Three stories*
> *Construction costs: $3,233,500*

Crawford Towers
> *150 Elderly units*
> *Five stories*
> *Construction cost: $3,688,000*

Brighton High-rise for the Elderly
        110 Elderly units
        10 stories
        Construction cost: $2,897,000

Conway Terrace
        248 units (195 new and 53 rehab.)
        Three stories and two stories
        Construction cost: $4,135,000

Lists like this are everywhere and they do you little or no good as you attempt to distinguish yourself against your competitor. Why are lists of this sort so ineffective as marketing tools? Because your competitor has submitted a proposal that contains a list that looks almost identical. Here is the list the competitor submitted:

Golden Sunshine Retirement Community
        96 Elderly units and community building
        Three stories
        Construction costs: $3,100,000

Cameron Place
        160 Elderly units
        Five stories
        Construction cost: $3,750,000

Guildwood High-rise for the Elderly
        95 Elderly units
        8 stories
        Construction cost: $2,530,000

Calloway Terrace Community
    195 units
    Three stories
    Construction cost: $3,895,000

As you can readily see, while the two firms have done different projects, for all intents and purposes, the two lists are identical. On the strength of these two lists, these firms have exactly the same qualifications.

The truth is that most of the firms you compete against are well qualified to do the work. You've done great projects. They've done great projects. For every project you can list, they can list another. In the 'battle of the lists' the two of you cancel each other out.

Perhaps even more serious is the impact this has on those making the consultant selection decision. Whenever you have to select between two apparently identical options, the only criteria left for making a decision is price! So, in this case who will win the project? The firm with the lower price. In the Battle of the Lists, low price wins every time.

There's another, perhaps greater weakness in the list game. Look at a typical project listing taken from a real proposal:

Project:	*Royal Heights Energy Improvements*
Client:	*Royal Management Corporation*
Const. Cost	*$285,000*
Description	*Energy efficient measures including window replacement, pipe wrapping, attic insulation furnace upgrades and caulking were a part of this overall remodeling of 174 Section 8 units and an Administration facility in 36 buildings.*

This description is totally 'neutral.' It relates the facts of what was done, but gives no hint as to the value the firm brought to the client and the project. Where are the lessons-learned that are being brought to the next project? Where are the victories and the difficulties overcome? Where are the real challenges that made you stop and have to really work to make that project the success it was?

Equally, if not more important, how does this project show that you are that 'ideal firm' you discovered that the client is seeking? How does this project push the 'hot buttons' you identified?

As written, this description could be of a project on which the consultant completely messed up or, conversely, one on which they saved the client an enormous amount of money. There is no hint given as to what the design firm contributed to the project.

So here's what you do.
Instead of writing boring, "just the facts, Ma'am" project descriptions, you're going to use the information and insight you gathered in your research and brainstorming to hard-wire

this project experience directly to the client's wish list. Let's go back to the example of brainstorming results we used in discussing cover letters.

The project is a new Medical Center addition and recall that your answers were these:

Hot Buttons
- Completing the project within 18 months
- Maintaining positive community relations
- Maintaining ongoing operations during construction
- Control over a very tight budget

Ideal Firm
- Located within 20 minutes of the project
- Willing to accept input of Board of Directors and doctors
- Full service firm with all in-house disciplines
- Project manager who has extensive medical center experience

Objections to your firm
- Located 100 miles away from the project   (true)
- Lacks in-house engineering staff   (true)
- PM has little medical center experience   (false)
- Not the firm we've always worked with   (true)

Competition
Acme Architects   + high quality contract documents
                - poor reputation for budget control

Ace Architects + strong project management
- reputation for poor client relations

Long & Short A/E + worked with client before
- high priced

A traditional description of a relevant project might look something like this:

Project: *Acme Medical Associates Office*
Client: *Acme Medical Associates, LLC*
Const. Cost *$1.3 million*
Description *Design of new medical office building to house a team of six doctors. Project included 10,000 square feet of office space on two floors with accommodation for a third floor addition in the future.*

Plenty of firms have done projects like this. From now on you are going to let the client really see the value you bring. This description will focus on the hot button of community relations and the 'potential objection' of your firm being 100 miles from the project site.

Project: *Acme Medical Associates Office*
Client: *Acme Medical Associates, LLC*
Description *This 10,000 square foot medical office was designed for a close-knit team of six doctors with strong ties to their community. In order to ease patient transition to the new location, our design team provided the doctors with a monthly 'update newsletter' to be mailed to their patient list. This kept patients informed and excited*

about the new office. To further reinforce the feeling of community we assigned Jim Travers, who had grown up in the adjacent neighborhood, as project architect.

Personal Profiles

You used to call them resumes. But don't do that anymore. A resume is the document you use when you're looking for a new employer. A personal profile is what you use when you're trying to persuade a client to retain your firm for a new project. The difference is in the detail and the emphasis that's given to the information.

Here is an example of an actual 'resume,' pulled from a proposal and typical of the sort you see in countless design firm proposals. (The name and identifying details have been changed.)

Mr. John Doe, P.E., A.I.C.P.
Manager of Municipal Engineering

Areas of Expertise
Traffic Engineering, transportation planning, storm water analysis, priority watershed planning, project management, capital improvement programming, utility system planning.

Education
M.S., Urban and Regional Planning,
University of South Carolina, 1978
B.S., Civil Engineering, Clemson University, 1974

Registration
Professional Engineer in Iowa (#345-1489) Illinois (#7890537590), Wisconsin (#38274585679) and Kansas (#2849573)

Professional Affiliations
   American Public Works Association
   American Planning Association
   American Institute of Certified Planners
   Institute of Transportation Engineers

Employment
   Smith & Jones Engineering

   City of Des Moines, IA

   City of Madison, WI

Experience
   Has extensive experience directed to municipalities for traffic engineering, utility design, comprehensive plan development, zoning and subdivision ordinances, transportation, buildings and recreational facilities. Has considerable experience in short- and long-range planning for communities of several thousand to one million people.

   Prepare and complete long-range studies of water supply, sewer, and collection systems and develop storm water management plans. Storm water analysis includes detention and sedimentation basins to reduce sediment flows. Has been project manager of numerous priority watershed studies and designs in the Midwest. Has provided project management and quality assurance for transportation projects including design for residential streets, major arterials, and industrial parks and studies related to traffic and corridors, needs, safety, and location. Also serves as city engineer for several communities and townships in the southern portion of the state.

Related Projects
  Sioux Highway
  Project manager for reconstruction of a half-mile section of road that included a water main, sewer interceptor and storm sewer.

  Matthews Road
  Project manager on a half-mile reconstruction of an arterial roadway under joint jurisdiction of two communities. Project involved a new water main, storm sewer and roadway.

  Broadway Corridor Traffic Study
  The City and the Community Development Authority developed a plan to redevelop the Turner St. Corridor from 51st Street to Highway 27. As a part of the development team, Smith & Jones was contracted to undertake a traffic study of the Turner St. Corridor to determine the impact of the proposed development. As a part of this work, made traffic projections of the new development, assessed impact on the current road network and recommended future improvements to the system.

  Broad River/Shining Creek Watershed
  This project involved six separate studies in three different communities in the metropolitan area. The watersheds studied ranged in area from 12 to 800 acres. As a result of the studies, eight separate Best Management Practices were approved for design and construction.

Did you actually read the whole thing? My guess is that, at best, you scanned it. More likely, you started into it, read a little, got bored quickly, and then jumped straight down to here where the text (hopefully) gets interesting again!

That's exactly what your clients do. Reading the colorless details of someone else's career is among life's more tedious tasks. And we avoid it whenever possible.

Since the point of the proposal is to 'persuade' the client to choose you, why not rebuild your profile to make it an exciting, vital and fascinating part of the persuasion process?

Fortunately, we can fine tune and focus Mr. Doe's profile using the research and brainstorming that you will have done. The project is a watershed study and came up with the following brainstorming answers:

Hot Buttons
- Long term recommendations for commercial development
- Contribution to existing GIS database
- Working closely with county engineering staff

Ideal Firm
- Extensive stormwater design experience
- Familiarity with local politics of development
- Success in community relations with small towns

Here's how Mr. Doe might assemble a personal profile targeted directly to this client.

Your Project Engineer

Mr. John Doe, P.E., A.I.C.P., will be the project engineer for your watershed study. With more than twenty years of 'lessons learned' from small municipalities like yours throughout the upper Midwest, John is a recognized leader in finding common ground between local commercial interests, long-range community planning and the needs of the natural environment.

- For the town of Podunk, a community similar in size to yours, John worked closely with the engineering staff to combine the data from the 400 acre watershed study with the town's ongoing effort to build a GIS database. The town engineer estimated the effort saved close to $10,000 in data collection costs.

- The Broad River/Shining Creek Watershed project involved six separate studies in three different communities. With strong pressure for commercial development, and each community working to attract business, John was required to balance the sometimes conflicting interests of local politicians, staff and commercial developers. His long-term design recommendations were praised by all concerned and eight separate Best Management Practices were approved for design and construction.

"John's ability to work productively with small towns was most appreciated. He kept us all working together."

James P. Gilmore, Mayor, Town of Podunk

- Since joining Smith & Jones Engineering 15 years ago, John has conducted 36 stormwater studies and designs -- more than any other engineer in the region. His recommendations have been valued by politicians, staff and developers and he has even been a speaker at the national conference of the American Planning Association.

Reference
Ms. Janice Woodcock
Planner, Town of Clearville
(123) 456-7890

Ms. Woodcock worked closely with John during the watershed study and can give insight into his ability to work with town engineering staff.

John was selected for this assignment from among our talented engineering staff because he, more than anyone else, combines the stormwater planning expertise with a keen understanding of the dynamics of development in smaller communities.

John is currently working on a similar study for Cooper County and will be available to begin work on your project on September 1.

Notice how this profile didn't mention anything about his experience in traffic studies or the design of recreational buildings. The content of this profile focused exclusively on those things that are up front in the client's mind. Should another project come up that concerns traffic engineering, John's profile will say little or nothing about watershed studies.

You'll also notice how this profile is considerably shorter and far easier and more pleasant to read. It actually tells 'stories' that are intriguing. The bottom line: this is a person that the client wants on their project team.

Additional Proposal Writing Tips
Telling Great Stories
Do you remember way back when you were four or five. You'd had your bath, you were all cozy in your pajamas and Mom

or Dad was tucking you into bed? Remember as you snuggled under the covers while they read you a bedtime bullet point list?

Of course you don't. What a ludicrous notion! No child would put up with something so crushingly boring as to be read a list! No, your Mom read you stories. She read stories because stories are interesting, they're entertaining, they have fascinating characters who face and overcome challenges. But most important, stories teach lessons. They have morals that allow us to see and understand things that we didn't before.

Stories are a whole lot more interesting and valuable as agents of communication than are lists. Lists are not only boring to read, they don't provide any insight into the value you brought to the project. Generic descriptions are, well, generic and fail to get anyone excited.

Fortunately, there are other ways to show your experience and the value you bring to your clients.

The RFP stated: *Please address your firm's approach to creative problem solving.*

The response could have been a generic description such as:

Acme Engineers is dedicated to bringing a creative approach to problem solving. We begin by assembling a team of experts who study the problem from as many angles as possible. We then convene a brainstorming session in which creative ideas from all participants are encouraged and recorded. The ideas are then ranked using a voting mechanism, which identifies the top five ideas.

Projects on which we've utilized creative problem solving include:...

Followed by the predictable, boring and uninspiring list.

Not very interesting, engaging or convincing. So how about something like this instead?

The Farmers Are Planting Drywall!

When Beaumont Health Systems wanted a new office building on their West Campus, they specified that the project should be LEED Certified. This had implications for the building, but also for the waste stream that every construction project generates. The goal was set at diverting at least 50% of the waste from the local landfills.

Never content to simply meet the goals, we set up an in-house contest with teams assigned to each component of the waste stream. Who could divert the largest volume of waste?

By the time we were finished, we'd diverted nearly 350 tons of concrete, brick and block from the landfill and crushed it off-site to be used for fill and other appropriate applications. We worked with the waste management company to begin a sorting process for the general trash, leading to waste diversion of close to 80%. But the winning team, with the most creative solution, had located a landscape supplier who took the gypsum from the old drywall to be ground up and resold as farm fertilizer.

The project is currently diverting 75% of the construction waste from the landfill, which earned the project two LEED credits, allowed Beaumont to leave a minimal impact on the environment and raised awareness within the construction workforce, Beaumont employees and the community at large.

A story like this ensures that the client will actually read it. Who, browsing through a proposal and coming across a headline like that, would not? Also, the story clearly demonstrated the firm's creative problem solving ability in a way that no generic description or list ever could. And that's all you need. No boring lists. No generic descriptions. Just an engaging tale of remarkable accomplishment. The kind you achieve every day.

Really bad photos
A picture is worth 1,000 words. But those words will say nasty things about your firm if you don't choose and use your images wisely.

I can't count the number of times I've seen photos included in proposals, presentations, on websites and even in printed brochures that are just plain awful. Heavily pixilated, out of focus and boring are the most common offenses. But there are other transgressions that border on the criminally dumb too.

Low resolution photos – even the least expensive cell phone today can capture a digital image that is capable of being blown up to billboard proportions. So why do I see so many photos that look more like an ancient Greek mosaic? If the digital image isn't large enough to blow up without pixilation, don't use it. Take it again at a higher resolution or find another.

Poorly composed photos – there are a few simple rules of visual composition that anyone can learn in about three minutes. Have good visual balance, don't cut off important elements of your image, find an angle that lets the light enhance the subject in the best way. Google 'how to take a good photo' and share the information around the office.

Boring photos – there is nothing the least bit engaging about a photo of a piece of PVC pipe lying in the bottom of a muddy trench. But that's what I encounter when I look at the project experience sheets from countless civil engineering firms. The other disciplines have their own versions of these predictable pics. Yes, it might be a photo of the project, but no one wants to look at a picture of an empty sidewalk on the side of the road! Find a stock photo of kids riding their bikes to school, instead.

Photos without people – the architects are the worst offenders on this one. It always seems that we wait until 5 AM on a Sunday to take the photo to make sure there isn't a living, breathing sentient being within five miles of the project! I know there are rules about signing waivers for people in photos, but get the staff from your office or hire your cousin to sit on the bench. The project was designed to accommodate humans—let's see a few populating it!

Photos without captions – flip through any magazine and you'll see that every photo has a caption. That's because we are too busy (or lazy) to read the articles. So we look at the pictures and read the captions. The client reviewing your proposal is no different. And don't have the caption simply say, "New 14-inch watermain along Main Street." Instead, let them tell a story: "Smith and Jones worked hard to keep the business owners along Main Street informed and up-to-date as the new watermain project progressed."

If you don't have compelling and engaging photos of the project, use some high quality, life-style photos that show people living the great life that your infrastructure project helps support. Or mix and match some life-style photos in with your more technical shots. There are many great stock photography websites that have high quality, royalty-free images at really low prices. Try istockphoto.com or fotolia.com.

Poor quality photos in your proposals, or in any of your marketing and business development efforts look unprofessional, amateurish and cheesy—not traits that make clients want to rush to hire your firm.

Ugly, ugly headshots

The debate has been going on as long as I can remember – should we use headshots in our resumes?

The answer is a loud and confident, "PERHAPS!"

But before we talk about when you should and should not include a headshot, let's set down a really strict rule: Pay a professional photographer to take HIGH QUALITY portraits.

I can't tell you how many times I've seen those really awful headshots included in proposals. You know them—the snapshots in which the subject was told to stand, facing the camera, back against a wall in a poorly lit hallway. Now smile!

The results make drivers license and passport photos look downright flattering!

The poor quality of these photos subconsciously translates to a poor perception of your firm, removes any sense of personality or intelligence from the individual and, one more time, looks just like the photos in your competitor's proposal.

A talented portrait photographer can create a photo in which the unique personality of the subject shines through. With creative lighting and non-traditional poses they can show anyone to be a fascinating individual that you'd like to meet. Ask them to be creative and don't be afraid of using the eye-catching results.

Now that you have decent photos, when should you use them? If the photos are high quality like we've just discussed, you can use them pretty much all the time. But there are two situations in which you should pause to consider.

If the client knows and has worked with the team members before and is likely to recognize the photo, by all means include the photos. The client will see the photo, recognize 'Bob' for the great Project Manager he is, and not even bother to read the profile.

But if the client isn't going to recognize the faces, you might want to consider leaving the photos out. Why? To avoid any risk that someone's facial features—the moustache, the long blond hair, the dark rimmed glasses—will subliminally remind the client of someone they don't particularly like. Yes, fair or not, we all make those instantaneous, subconscious connections that lead to preconceived notions. Do yourself and the client a favor by avoiding any chance of that happening.

Headshots can add some life and personality to an otherwise dull personal profile. But only if that photo has some life and personality in it.

Testimonials
A testimonial is a statement from an existing client, who has

nothing to gain by it, endorsing your services. They are recommending that one of their peers purchase your services.

Testimonials are among the most powerful marketing and sales tools you can use and I like to sprinkle them liberally throughout the various sections of the proposal. Put another way, your clients are much better at marketing you that you are. So use them as often as you can.

Every firm has letters of recommendation. They are often photocopied and included at the end of your proposal. The problem is, in that location, they're never read. A client, with insufficient time to read your proposal, scans through the document and finds a page that is obviously a photocopy of an old letter that recommends your services. They mentally note that you have clients who are willing to recommend you (Who doesn't?) and they continue to turn pages without ever actually reading the letter.

To get the most value from the reference and testimonial letters you have, you need to extract the most valuable statements from the letter and make them easily accessible to the reader.

Here is an actual testimonial letter from a client. Again, identifying information been changed.

June 25, 2009

John Q. Smith Construction Co.
123 4th Street,
Yourtown, ST 12345

Attn: Mr. John Smith
         Construction Executive

Re: NewTowne Office Development

Gentlemen:

We refer to our Construction Management Agreement with you dated September 18, Article 9.8, Substantial Completion, and to the fully executed Certificate of Substantial Completion for Level 5 (six pages dated June 3, copy attached). We forward you copy of this certificate to you with great pleasure. We congratulate you and your staff, both in the field and in the main office, for achieving this first substantial completion milestone at Level 5.

Your company's on-time delivery of the completed fifth floor, at a level of cleanliness, fit and finish seldom seen in our industry, is an achievement for which you should all be proud. Please extend our congratulations and thanks to all of your staff involved.

As a result of your achievement, we are pleased to look forward to your equally successful and on-time completion of the remaining areas of the building. Please do not hesitate to ask if there is anything we can do to assist you in achieving your goals. All of us here at NewTown Properties maintain genuine enthusiasm working with you to successfully complete all areas.

Again, congratulations to all of you.

Sincerely,
Michael Jones

If you managed to wade through the first paragraph and hadn't fallen asleep, you would discover a real marketing jewel in the second paragraph. But there is little likelihood that a client would get that far. You will also notice that the letter is dated, 2009. Five years is the longest shelf life of any testimonial letter.

Instead of simply photocopying the letter and inserting it in your proposal, pull out the really good stuff and use it where it has the most impact. When you do this, you discover that this letter contains at least four separate testimonials. Additionally, these individual sentences are separated from the date of the letter and become timeless.

Hot button is schedule:
"We congratulate you and your staff, both in the field and in the main office, for achieving this first substantial completion milestone."

Hot button is quality work:
"Your company's on-time delivery of the completed fifth floor, at a level of cleanliness, fit and finish seldom seen in our industry, is an achievement for which you should all be proud."

Hot button is client relations:
"Please extend our congratulations and thanks to all of your staff involved."

"All of us here at NewTown Properties maintain genuine enthusiasm working with you."

Hot button is long-term relationship
"As a result of your achievement, we are pleased to look forward to

your equally successful and on-time completion of the remaining areas of the building."

These testimonials can be used anywhere, in any proposal where you want to make a powerful impact and reinforce a point you have discovered in your research and brainstorming.

Don't leave the testimonials to languish in fifth generation photocopies of letters at the back of the proposal. They'll never be read! Instead, pull out the really great statements and spread them throughout your proposal. Include them in personal and team profiles, in project approach statements, in your cover letter and in your project descriptions.

Testimonials are one of the most powerful 'persuasion tools' you have. Use them

7.3   MAKING PRESENTATIONS
Getting Ready for your Presentation

Your client has carefully reviewed all the qualifications—education, experience, approach, and has satisfied herself that each of the remaining five firms has the technical capability of doing this job. The project will be designed and built and it will work.

How does she sort through these remaining five?

Let's take a moment and drift back to the chapter on Business Development, where we talked about shopping. If you recall, we said that a client, when looking to purchase professional design services, doesn't have the advantage of trying out your firm before you do the work. They have to take a leap of faith that your firm is the right one and that they've made a good decision.

That's whey they go through this rigorous process and ask these multiple questions in different formats and venues. Because, at the end of the day, the only thing your client has got to go on is that moment when you look him in the eye and shake his hand and say, "I'm going to look after you.

That's why, when you get to the presentation stage, the client needs to be able to ask tough questions in person. They can tell a great deal about you by the way you answer. It's that trust and sense of confidence that clients are looking for and you need to be able to provide that in your interview.

So the objective in an interview or presentation is to provide an opportunity for personal, face-to-face communication that allows the client to have confidence in the decision they are about to make.

In stark contrast, have you ever had the misfortune of serving on a review panel or selection committee? This isn't a privilege, it's a sentence! All the presentations run together, they all look and sound the same, and by the time it's over you can't remember or distinguish one from another. You're fast asleep if not brain dead.

Typical Presentations
How do we typically go about developing a presentation? They inevitably start with

Click here to add Title

Click here to add Text

Actually, more often than we don't even start there. We pull up the last winning presentation that we did, click '*Save As,*' and then start changing dates and names.

But you don't want your client getting bored from just reading your bullet points. With PowerPoint we can put in pictures or clever diagrams. PowerPoint then goes even further and asks which background you'd like to use? Then it provides dozens of ready-made backgrounds and color schemes.

And if you're not satisfied with the options that comes with the software, there's been an entire culture built up around making PowerPoint even easier for you. Go online and Google

'PowerPoint Backgrounds' and you'll discover thousands of them waiting for you.

With all due respect to the people who have worked hard to create this supporting material, how dumb do you think your clients would have to be to decide that they will hire the team that had the blue color scheme instead of the green one? Or to have any notion that, 'you had that attractive background so we'll hire you.'

Is there somewhere on the face of this planet, a client that is so stupid as to say, 'Oh, let's hire them. They had a background with lines that sort of looked like circuit boards. They must be technically competent!'

Your clients are very smart, savvy, sophisticated people.

The problem with PowerPoint is that it has been designed as a tool that is convenient for the presenter. It has not been designed as a tool that is convenient for the audience.

And it truly does make a presenter's life easy. This is a great tool for organizing your thoughts: Click here to add title. Click here to add text. Add a diagram. And snap! you've got a presentation. Then, to make things even more convenient, you've got all your cheat notes right up there on the screen so you don't have to remember anything. You can simply stand there and read to your audience!

But... Think again about your objectives in a presentation. If, in fact, you could accomplish those objectives by simply reading your client a document, why don't you just send them an email that they can read for themselves?

Because that's not what you're trying to accomplish.

Preparing Your Presentation

Before you begin getting ready for your next presentation I want you to ask yourself this question:

> *"If I can assume that they will leave this presentation remembering one thing and only one thing, what would I like that thing to be?"*

Because the truth is that that's all they will remember. At best they'll remember one thing that you said. And you need to figure out what that one thing needs to be. In other words, what is the story that needs to be told?

When you're getting ready for your presentation, don't ever begin by firing up PowerPoint, don't ask how many slides, don't ask how many bullets per slide and don't ask what the background should be.

Instead, start with a blank wall, a pad of Post-It notes and a Sharpie. Whenever I'm asked to help out with a presentation, or developing a 'win strategy,' this is where I begin. And we start asking questions:

'Tell me about this client.'
'What's keeping him awake at night?'
'What drives her?'
'What are the drivers on this project?

Go back to your answers to the brainstorming questions you asked before you wrote the proposal. Go back, also, to the research you conducted in the Go/No Go decision process.

You begin preparing your presentation with another, although different, brainstorming process. This one lets you think freely and capture any and all ideas, no matter how wild and crazy. The Post-It notes are your idea-capturing tools. Start by simply brainstorming, writing each idea on its own sticky note, and sticking it on the wall.

"Here's a major point we'll want to make!"
"Here's a secondary point that would support it."
"Here's an anecdote we might tell to illustrate it."
"This hero story would really show how we go above and beyond."

As you think of similar, supplementary or related ideas, write them on more notes, stick them up, move them around, group them, rearrange them and modify them. Slowly a story will begin to emerge that clearly communicates how you're going to tackle this project to best serve this client.

You might be familiar with the concept of a storyboard. Movie makers use them to sketch out the elements and sequence of the story they're going to tell. They create some rough visuals that they intend to use to help tell the story. It's by no means the finished product but it's a fast, flexible tool that can change easily.

When you're brainstorming and building your storyboard identify the key points that you have to get across. What is your main message and what are the main elements of your message?

Don't try to list a dozen points. At best you'll be able to make three. More often than not you'll be able to effectively make one. Then answer this question:

"Why should the client care about what I'm saying?"

Here's a sobering thought: When you get up to do your presentation, your client has just sat through five other interviews. Their brain is numb from the experience and they're wondering, "Why should I care about this?" as you drone on about more lists of projects you've done for other people. And all the client is doing while you're talking is doodling on a piece of paper because their brain has left the building.

Every point you plan to make must have direct and relevant importance to this client. If you can't be completely clear as to why it's important, it's a good clue that you should simply leave out that point. It doesn't need to be made.

PowerPoint is NOT Your Presentation
There is a psychological concept known as 'cognitive overload.' In essence it says that the human brain is like one of those plastic 2-liter Coke bottles. It will actually hold quite a bit, but the opening is rather small and you can only get so much in at a time.

Imagine setting an empty one of those bottles on the ground and then trying to pour a pail full of water into the Coke bottle. How much of the water do you suppose would actually end up in the bottle? And how much would end up being splashed all over the ground?

When we communicate we're trying to pour our knowledge into our audience's brains so that they say, 'oh, wow! I understand it. I want that!' But when we use communication techniques that induce cognitive overload, most of the content of what you're saying simply spills out all over the ground.

In developing an effective presentation our goal should be to provide information in a way that maximizes the audience's ability to process and remember it. But it turns out that one of the least effective ways to accomplish this, the way that induces cognitive overload most quickly, is to have information come to you simultaneously in both written and spoken form.

Which is exactly what PowerPoint (used in the intended manner) does. When you have a screen full of bullet points, which the presenter is reading aloud while the audience simultaneously reads them silently, nothing sticks.

Remember that your objective is to make a personal connection; to communicate well enough that you connect on a personal, even an emotional level.

What are the dynamics of a typical PowerPoint presentation? First, everyone is sitting, facing the screen. Second, the presenter is either standing off in a dark corner, or standing in front of the audience but with his back to them, and everyone is reading together. The presenter out loud, the audience silently.

David A. Stone | Gail Hulnick

Fundamental point:
Whatever is up on the wall in your slides or your boards or
whatever props you might have is not your presentation.
You are the presentation.

Let's repeat that: whatever you have up on the wall is not the presentation. That is simply there to reinforce, augment, decorate and supplement the message that you, personally, as a human being are bringing to that audience so that you can connect with them.

If you can rely on the words on the wall to convey the message, then save everyone the hassle and just send a memo. If that would successfully communicate your message, then a presentation is an inappropriate medium to use.

But if a memo won't suffice, let's make sure you design and deliver a presentation that accomplishes the goals you want.

Timeless Wisdom

I was going through some old files and came across a memo that had been written more than 30 years ago. The author was a design firm Principal who had just "sat on the other side of the table." In other words, he had just experienced what it's like to be a client trying to select a design firm. His advice and encouragement to the other members of his firm is as good and on-target as it gets.

I spent all day yesterday listening to four joint venture firms give presentations for their services. It drilled home once again that good business development is essential if we are to sell work. In the Olympics there might be 18 inches difference between first and last place runners; and all the losers could easily win races elsewhere.

220

We are up against increasingly stiff competition. We're competing against people who really understand good marketing techniques, good sales, and good presentations. We've got to be outstanding to close that last 18 inches.

Here are some thoughts that occurred to me yesterday. We've discussed them all in the past, but I wanted to re-emphasize them to you.

1. *Make sure we understand what the client wants.*
   You can't find that just by reading the RFP. You've got to talk to the people who are doing the hiring. Those people are usually available. I was surprised yesterday at how few people talked to me or the other members of the interview committee before the interview. We were all available for questions.

2. *Include the buyer benefits.*
   Most of the presenters told us what they were going to do. But they didn't emphasize what the benefit to us would be. Sometimes we were able to infer the benefit; sometimes we couldn't. A few of the better presenters described their services in simple, declarative sentences, and then explained the benefits that would accrue to us if we hired them to provide those services.

3. *Prepare and rehearse*
   It was clear that some of the firms had spent time preparing for us, and some of them had not. The ones that prepared were well organized. They seemed relaxed and unconfused. The ones that hadn't prepared and rehearsed stumbled all over themselves, corrected one another and missed the mark.

4. *Don't talk about yourself too much.*

Several of the companies failed miserably because they just told us all about themselves and what they had done. We'd already read all about that in their proposals. What we wanted to know was how they were going to do our job. The companies that came out on top were the ones that spent all their time talking about how they were going to do things for us.

5. *Excitement and innovation sure help.*
    The firms that came out on top were those that clearly were excited by the opportunity, and had innovative approaches. It was clear who had thought the job through and who came in with their canned "we're big and this is the way we do it" approach. The companies that sold their traditional services failed. Those that met the unique needs of the project succeeded.

Delivering Your Presentation

Scientists pretty much universally agree that, about 13.7 billion years ago, something rather large happened. As one author summed it up, "Prior to that moment there was nothing; during and after that moment there was something: our universe."

Prior to your presentation, there is nothing. After you give your presentation, things should have changed. The client has made the decision to hire you. The audience has a newfound respect for your knowledge and insight.

The best way to launch your presentation is with a big, banging, smack-me-between-the-eyes opening. Your opening 60 seconds are like gold. Treat them carefully and extract the highest possible value from them.

Martin Luther King, Jr. opened his 'I have a dream speech' with, "I am happy to join with you today in what will go down in history as the greatest demonstration for freedom in the history of our nation."

JFK opened his first inaugural address by saying, "We observe today not a victory of party, but a celebration of freedom."

When you open your mouth to begin your next presentation, make sure it's with a really big bang.

I devour books voraciously and I recently came across a gem: *Public Speaking As Listeners Like It!*, by Richard C. Borden. It's old, long out of print and, based on the sensibilities of 1935, as politically incorrect as you can get. (e.g., It would appear that, in 1935, only men gave or listened to speeches!)

But once through all the quaint period issues, the book makes some fabulous points, as pertinent to your presentation today as they were then. I particularly like 'ol Richard's advice on opening a speech or presentation:

In the first section of your speech—start a fire! Your speech is not well organized unless you kindle a quick flame of spontaneous interest in your first sentence.

When you rise to make a speech, do not picture your audience as waiting with eager eyes and bated breath to catch your message.

Picture it, instead, as definitely bored—and distinctly suspicious that you are going to make this situation worse. Picture your

David A. Stone | Gail Hulnick

listeners as looking uneasily at their watches, stifling yawns and giving vent to a unanimous 'HO HUM!'

The first sentence of your speech must crash through your audience's initial apathy. Don't open your speech on Safety by saying: 'The subject which has been assigned me is the reduction of traffic accidents.' Say, instead: 'Four hundred and fifty shiny new coffins were delivered to this city last Thursday.'

Mr. Borden is absolutely right. Your audience, or the selection panel for your interview is not sitting on the edges of their seats, waiting to hear your every word. They are anticipating another boring, monotonous speaker with an endless supply of PowerPoint bullets. When you open with, "Good morning. We're really pleased to have this opportunity to present to you today...' they know that there is a pleasant snooze in their immediate future.

Predictable, boring and commonplace are not the ingredients of a 'Holy Cow!' presentation. Think of the opening sequence of any James Bond film. It puts you on the edge of your seat from the first frame and keeps you there through the entire movie. Snoozing is not an option!

Yes, it might feel a little uncomfortable to open with a statement that is controversial, provocative and totally unexpected. But it will light a fire under the seats of your audience and have them hanging on every word that follows.

Is Anyone Paying Attention?
Let's talk for a minute about the dynamics of your audience.

Think back to the last presentation you attended. Maybe it lasted an hour. Did you maintain absolute, unflinching, concentrated focus through the entire presentation? Of course you didn't. Your mind drifts. It wanders off to other thoughts. Maybe things going on at work, things you have to remember to take care of at home, an errand you have to run on your way home that evening. Regardless, your mind wanders all over. The human mind is an enormously difficult thing to control.

As your presentation goes on the level of attention that the audience is paying changes. The good news is that it changes in ways that are highly predictable. At the beginning of any presentation or speech given by anyone the audience is paying a high level of attention. They are thinking, 'this is new, I haven't heard this person speak before, is there something I'm going to learn, what's of value to me?' Early on they are going to be paying close attention.

However, once the speaker is into the presentation, the audience's attention level falls off. Quite steeply actually. As your presentation rolls on, the audience members are off to many different places—everywhere except here listening to you! Then, as they sense you are coming to an end—"it was a 30 minute presentation, it's been 25 minutes, I guess they'll be wrapping up soon"—they start paying attention because they know they can pick up the gist in your summary. And you always oblige by giving a summary.

A good speech writer knows how this dynamic works and they will insert what we call 'attention spikes.' They will write a joke into the speech, which brings everyone back. Or they will tell an interesting anecdote that will bring the audience back to the speaker. But only temporarily since we know they'll drift off again.

Knowing that the dynamics of audience attention level work this way, how is the typical presentation designed?

When the presenter is first introduced, audience attention levels are very high. But most presenters waste this valuable attention by talking about things that don't matter:

> 'Good morning. I'm really pleased to have this opportunity to present to you today. I'd like to take a moment to tell you a little bit more about our firm and allow you to get to know us personally. Before we get started I'd like to tell you about the history of our company. We've been in business since 1932. Our firm was founded by George Founder and we've grown steadily since. We now have 10 offices in three states...'

As that boring presenter drones on, imagine that you're watching the dial on an Attention-O-Meter attached to the audience. It's falling fast! They are drifting off. And they're drifting off just as the presenter is about to head into the meat of his presentation. The audience has left the room. They're gone and not listening to all the really important things he has to say. They miss the punch line.

Then, when the audience does return its attention in time for the close, what do we typically do? We wrap up by saying, ' I'd like to thank you again for allowing us to be here today and reinforce just how important this project is to us and tell you how committed we are to your satisfaction.'

The presentation opened with trite statements. Then it closed with trite statements and all the good stuff was put into the part where the audience was missing. It is any wonder that we have so many snoozers during a presentation?

Lincoln didn't begin the Gettysburg address by introducing himself and he didn't close by thanking the audience for their time and attention. A good pitcher will always lead with his best pitch. Let's learn the lesson.

Keeping Your Audience's Attention
You likely know that either first or last in the order of presentations offers an advantage. The firms that present first and last are more likely to stand out and stick in the mind of the client. But the same rule applies within the confines of your own presentation.

Trial lawyers have always known that, in order to persuade a jury, they can rely on two principles: the doctrines of *primacy* and *recency*. Primacy says that you should always lead off with your strongest statement. This catches your audience off guard and leaves a dramatic and indelible first impression. Recency says that you should go out with a bang and leave a lasting impression that stays with the client long after your presentation is over.

From this you might conclude that the very beginning and the very end of your presentation are the best times to communicate your most important information. And you'd be right. This is an opportunity for you to gain some real advantage.

Here are some samples of opening lines and themes you can use in a smack-me-between-the-eyes opening. When I say 'opening line,' that's exactly what I mean. Don't start with, 'good morning,' or 'thank you for inviting us here,' or any other line that your competitor is sure to use. Head straight into the good stuff.

If the client's key hot button is:

Schedule, you might start with:

> *"This morning we are going to show you how your bridge reconstruction project can actually be completed in less time than you anticipated. We have analyzed the project in depth and we have discovered at least six areas where time can be saved. We are going to share these ideas with you today."*

Technical issues:

> *"As you streamline and automate the city's water filtration and sewage disposal system, you have wisely chosen to integrate their control with the use of a SCADA system. In our meeting today, our chief programmer is going to review the system we intend to design for you to make sure you fully understand how the system will work, what safeguards are built in and how your operators will be trained in the use of the system. We will be illustrating our discussion with case studies from the SCADA systems we have designed and installed for Greenbury and Harpers Mills."*

The approvals process:

> *"This project would be a piece of cake if it weren't for the challenge of gaining EPA approval. In our presentation this afternoon, we are going to focus almost exclusively on the process we will use to apply to and then negotiate with the EPA for your VIP (Very Important Permit)."*

Construction costs:

> *"We are all aware of the instability of construction costs in this market no one is more concerned about controlling them on your behalf than we at Smith & Jones. In our interview this morning we are going to show you the many techniques we are going to use to ensure that, throughout the design and contract document process, construction costs are estimated and ensured as closely as possible."*

Compare any of these bold openings with the boring old, "We are pleased to be presenting to you today..." Any client, with those hot buttons front and center in their mind, will sit up and pay attention.

But as you recall, our imaginary Attention-O-Meter also drops dramatically during the middle of the interview. By injecting an item of interest, a story or introducing a physical prop, you can reclaim the attention you're losing. 'Attention spikes' are verbal or visual devices that bring a group back together. For example:

"In summary..."

Don't wait until the end of the show. You can summarize as often as you like. Each time, you will get everyone's attention back because they don't want to miss the important point.

"Now I'm going to show you..."

Words like this indicate that something new is about to happen. They want to see if it has relevance for them so they will tune back in while you introduce the new topic.

"I know you'll appreciate this…"

This speaks directly to your client's search for direct benefits. If you say they will appreciate something, they don't want to miss out.

"Here's something you may not have known…"

This appeals to the natural curiosity that is embedded in human nature. Everyone is bound to sit up and pay attention when you open a paragraph with this phrase.

"Let's take a look at…"

This brings you and the audience together in a joint activity. You are also giving the audience an instruction which they are happy to follow.

Your first obligation in any presentation is to answer the client's question: "What's in it for me?" If you can't do that at the very beginning, you won't have their interest in the first place and you won't be able to regain what you never had.

Engaging Multiple Senses
In a typical presentation you involve the audience's sight and hearing. But the remaining three senses are rarely activated. To the degree that you can involve more of the senses, you will be more memorable.

What can you bring to your next presentation that you can pass around for the client to touch and hold? How about a jar of waste water? A brick sample? An old section of rusty pipe that you've dug up from a previous utility project? A soil sample? A concrete core? There are so many tangible 'artifacts' from your work that you could bring to a presentation to not only engage an additional sense, but to bring what you do closer to their experience. And to make your presentation more memorable.

And when you bring that concrete core, drop it on the table so they actually experience the weight and sound of the concrete. When you pass the jar of wastewater around, invite them to take a sniff and take away the memory of the power of what you do when you transform that wastewater into clean water that can be safely put back into the river.

By engaging additional senses you drive home the points you are making, keep the audience involved and paying attention and ensure that they're not about to forget your presentation.

A primary goal of your presentation is to be memorable. To the degree that you can engage taste, and touch, and smell in addition to hearing and sight, then you achieve that goal. Because props are tactile, your audience will remember the smell and the feel and the weight of those things that you placed in their hands. Now they have a much more vivid sense of what you're going to do for them. They know how much the components weigh and they have a sense of how they fit together. And they start to remember.

The more we can engage these senses, the more memorable your presentation becomes. Which is why I like to bring stuff that you can touch, and smell, and once in a while, that you can taste. If the presentation is at three o'clock in the afternoon I've brought chocolate chip cookies. "Here, it's mid afternoon, we're all dragging our butts a little by now, have a cookie.' I've even done presentations at 5:00 in the afternoon where I've even brought beer.

But don't let me hear, 'hey, he said he brought beer and it worked. We should always bring beer!' Is that always appropriate? NO! Absolutely not. But in that situation, with that client, at that time, it made sense and it worked.

I will also be the first to confess that I've had wild ideas and said, 'Oh! Let's do this! And had it blow up in my face completely.' But I'll also be the first to tell you that I would much rather go down in flames and come dead last because we tried something bold, than I would come second. Coming second is as easy as falling off a log. Coming first is hard. Coming dead last is also hard. But I'd rather come dead last than come second.

At all times remember that our objective is not to be cute or gimmicky. Our objective is enormously serious and our approach is based on the art of communication. How do I get an idea that's in my head successfully transferred to your head? We use these techniques, not because they're unusual or novel. We use them because they can more effectively communicate your ideas and more permanently stick in your client's head.

Presenting on camera
You normally find yourself presenting in person to a committee or selection panel, but there are two important settings where on-camera skill becomes a factor in marketing your services — you on the short list, and you on YouTube.

These days it's a regular occurrence for clients to put the presentations of their short-listed proponents on video, particularly in the public sector. If your presentation is going to be recorded you need to use every skill you have and then crank it up a level. The camera will exaggerate every habit, every vocal tic, every questionable wardrobe choice you make.

The second scenario has more to do with your brand-building efforts than your sales and business development. YouTube should be one of the social networks that you consider seriously as part of your branding tools. The price is right and the 'reach' can be incredible.

When you rehearse for a presentation, (you're going to do at least three rehearsals and practice your responses to unscripted questions, right?), do it on camera. Even if it's somebody's Smartphone and you only view it on a four-inch screen afterward, you'll see improvements and corrections you'll be able to make the next time.

The most common problem that we see is bad eye contact and control. The camera picks up on eye movement in a way that's almost spooky. Perhaps you have a habit of flicking your gaze from left to right or even if the eye movement is a result of stress from facing the lens or from the high stakes of the presentation itself. At best this comes across as a lack of confidence and maturity. At worst, you look shifty and dishonest.

Here are the top three tips you can adopt to make the most of your time in the spotlight.

1. Know your material backward and forwards because if you are at all unprepared you won't be able to fake it.

2. During your rehearsals, figure out your best posture, gestures, stance, and facial expressions, practice them and use them.

3. Find your best stress management tools, apply them, and work on developing your comfort level with the camera to the point where people comment that you look totally at ease.

You don't have to be a brilliant actor or even a good one, but you do have to avoid the wooden, amateurish delivery that most untrained people bring to video.

Voice, accents and up-talk

Before you go on camera, and even before you step in front of a live audience, find someone who will give you a straightforward assessment of your vocal impact. Be realistic—very few people have a voice that will put them into a professional broadcast career. But there are things you can do if your voice is shrill, if you have a speech impediment, or if you speak in a monotone. If you don't ask, you may never know what's getting in your way.

Accents are a special situation. People are often reluctant to say much about your accent, even if asked directly, because they fear their intentions will be misunderstood. But let's assume we're here to work on developing skills that are useful for business—and the ability to communicate is one of the vital ones.

No one is asking you to deny your country of origin or to back away from business presentation opportunities. But if you do speak with an accent, survey a few people on their reactions to your speaking style. Do they notice your accent? Does it interfere with them comprehending you? Do you speak too quickly? (Often this is the simple solution for speakers who find their accent is a drawback). Can you use humor at the outset of the presentation (and sometimes, as part of your 'elevator speech') in a way that will put others at their ease?

'Uptalk' is an all-to-common speaking habit that many listeners find annoying? It also frequently identifies the speaker as young, poorly educated, and lacking experience? It's one of the biggest barriers to advancement for young women and many of them don't know it, because no one will tell them?

By now you've figured out what 'uptalk' is and why you should work to avoid it. (If you haven't, read the previous paragraph again.) Along with quite a few other bad cadence, intonation and phrasing habits, uptalk is born of and spread by television.

Awareness is the first step to breaking this habit. Record yourself speaking. Ask friends to point out each time they hear you turning simple sentences into questions that leave the listener wondering, "Am I supposed to answer that?!"

These habits can be altered with a little practice. When speaking, try raising your chin slightly as you begin a sentence and bringing it back down as you complete it. Slightly is the important word here; you don't want to look like a bobble-head doll. But that tiny movement is enough to make you aware of what your voice is doing and help you break the uptalk habit.

Becoming aware of your breathing also works. Inhale when you are starting to make your point and exhale when you are finishing it. Breath control is also a terrific tool for developing other areas of vocal control and presentation skills.

Presentation skills, whether in person or on camera, are vital for anyone who occupies or aspires to a leadership position in a professional design firm. If you want to be taken seriously by leaders, decision-makers, managers and owners you should analyze your voice, the words you use and the way you say them.

The most wonderful thing you can do with PowerPoint
It will spin, twist and magically appear. It will directly insert online video clips, embed Flash animations and put flaming heads on the photos you've chosen. I wouldn't be surprised if the next release will remove those stubborn stains on your carpet.

But there is one thing that PowerPoint can do that is more powerful than any of these: It can turn off.

Right smack in the middle of your presentation, you can turn it off and talk, just talk to your audience. Amazing!

First let me tell you how you do this. If you're running the program from a keyboard, press the 'B' key and the screen will turn black. Press the 'W' key and the screen will turn white. Press either key again and the slide you turned off is back on the screen. If you're using a remote, there's often a button that will turn off the slide.

Now let's talk about why you should use this feature.

The reason you're making a presentation is to connect with your audience. To engage with them in a way that gets them excited, persuades them, educates them or leaves them motivated to get up and do something different. If your purpose was merely to convey information, an email or a memo is probably a better idea.

No one has ever been excited, motivated or persuaded by simply watching PowerPoint slides click by. It takes a real live human being to engage an audience. Abraham Lincoln, JFK, Martin Luther King, Jr. and Winston Churchill never used PowerPoint, and likely wouldn't have even if it had been available. The best presenters, the best speakers, the best teachers and preachers know that the only way to connect with an audience is to engage them with eye contact, body language, vocal expression and genuine enthusiasm. None of those things can happen if we're all reading bullet points together.

Your slides are mostly decoration, augmentation and back-up to what you're saying. As long as they're up on the screen, the audience is distracted from the real presentation, which is you. Never forget that YOU, not your slides, are the presentation.

So, every once in a while, turn your slides off. Then tell a story, ask a question, invite comments from the audience and engage in some dialogue. They'll remember that long after they've forgotten your slides.

8

CLIENT SERVICE

What's it like to shop at your store?

There used to be a grocery store chain in Virginia called Ukrop's. They were in business for more than 70 years until, a few years back, the owners took their well-deserved rewards in a buy-out. While they were operating, they had an almost mythical reputation for customer service.

I never got to shop there myself, but over the years I've met many people who did and they invariably had their own, personal service stories to tell:

> *I stopped in around dinnertime, having just picked up my 18-month-old from daycare. She'd neither eaten nor had a recent diaper change and was wailing up a storm. I pushed my cart into one aisle and saw an employee – probably late teens – stacking shelves. When he heard the screaming baby, he dropped the soup cans and ran out of the aisle. But not 20 seconds later, he was back. He'd run to the bakery department, grabbed a cookie and*

asked if it might help her feel better!

I was in search of chopped walnuts for my annual Christmas baking spree. The shelf was empty and the grocery manager confirmed they were out of stock. But then he said, "Carry on with your shopping. I'll take care of this." I then watched as he went to the front of the store, nabbed one of the employees bagging groceries, handed him a $10 bill and told him to run across the street (to a competitor's store!) and buy a bag of walnuts. By the time I was in the checkout line, the young man was back, handed me the bag of nuts with a smile and wished me a Merry Christmas!

Before we moved to Dallas, we lived in Virginia and always shopped there. About six months after the move (when the Postal Service stopped forwarding their advertising flyers) I received a personal note from the President. The note said how it had come to his attention that we'd left the Richmond area; how he wanted to thank us for our patronage during the years we'd lived there; how he wished us the best of luck in our new home in Texas and how, if we ever returned to Virginia, he'd love to welcome us back to Ukrop's.

WOW!

There are some interesting take-aways here. First, everyone I met was an enthusiastic, unpaid member of the store's marketing department. They loved to tell their stories and recruit new customers. Second, they all agreed that it was more expensive to shop there, but absolutely worth it. Finally, it doesn't get much more commoditized than chopped walnuts. But the fantastic service was enough to break that price sensitivity.

Every one of us has had the experience of walking into a store with the intention of buying a new shirt, blouse, pair of shoes…

whatever. And then, not three minutes later, walking back out of the store having decided that not only are we never going to shop there again, we're going to make it a personal mission that no one else ever does either.

And we've also had the opposite experience —walking into the store expecting to buy a shirt, and coming out two hours later with an entire wardrobe.

Both those decisions had nothing to do with price or product availability. They were both driven by the way you were treated by the staff in the store. In the first instance they were too busy chatting to realize you were there and their body language shouted that they weren't interested in serving you. In the second store, you were made to feel like you were the most important person on earth, nothing was too much trouble and the clerk had all the time in the world for you.

So, what's it like to shop at your AE store?

Your customers walk in and order "Ten pounds of engineering please!" Or, "Do you have any size 10 architecture?" Of course we're being facetious but we have to ask what that experience is like? How are your clients greeted and treated while they're in your 'store?' What is it like to phone into your office?

You've had the experience of phoning a company and then being made to feel like you were a disturbance rather than a customer. And you've also had the opposite experience—being made to feel like they had been waiting for your call. All these little things add up to a big impression that makes a customer want to stay or to look elsewhere.

A large store chain may spend millions on advertising. (You spend thousands on your marketing programs.) The store carefully ensures that the shelves are stocked with the right inventory. (You make sure your staff is trained and equipped to effectively do your work.) They continually rework the look of the store so it appeals to potential customers. (You massage your website and your proposals to make them more appealing.) All this work brings new customers in the door.

Then it's up to the store clerk.

In many ways, your project managers and project delivery teams are like those store clerks. Your firm may work tirelessly to attract new clients. You may spend thousands chasing and winning a particular project. But it's only when the client has the chance to experience the service available from the project delivery team, will they decide whether or not to 'shop at your store' again.

You've got a lot of competitors and they all sell the same chopped nuts that you do. What's it like to shop at your store?

Keeping clients for life

You've heard it many times before—landing a new client costs 10, 25, 100 times more than keeping an old one. No one agrees on the actual multiple but everyone agrees that it's MUCH more expensive. And losing a client costs you all the overhead and marketing you've invested in landing them in the first place.

Keeping your clients happy in a long-term relationship is just good business —higher profits, lower overheads, less stress and the peace of mind of a continuing supply of profitable work.

In these days of intense competition, your clients are taking some very hard looks at why they are continuing to work with the same consultants and suppliers and whether or not they should switch. It takes a lot more than loyalty to keep a client today!

There are six practices you can adopt to ensure your clients stay around and continue to come back to you for project after project.

1. Provide over-the-top customer service
Every one of your competitors can produce the same great technical work that you can. That's why we call them 'competitors!' So why should a client choose to hire you instead of them? Over-the-top customer service will give you a competitive edge that technical expertise and even low price can never overcome. You've experienced great customer service (just not often enough) and you know that you're willing to pay extra for it.

Imagine for a minute that you own and operate a store. But instead of clothes or groceries, your store sells engineering. What is it like to shop at your store? What do customers experience when they come in? How are they greeted? Are they made to feel wanted and welcome? How are they treated by the staff? What are they thinking when they leave?

What can you do to improve that experience and make it more pleasant and memorable?

2. Seek regular feedback

The idea of seeking out regular, reliable and candid feedback from clients is simultaneously exciting and terrifying. It feels great to get the "attaboys" and the glowing testimonials when things go well, but what kind of feedback do you want or get when you screw up? How often do you actively seek your clients' opinions about what you do well and what you do poorly? More importantly, what do you do with those opinions when they're given?

The first lesson in looking for client feedback is a word of caution. Regardless of how you learn what clients think about your firm, once they've shared their thoughts they fully expect you're going to do something about it. If you're not prepared to act on the suggestions and make real changes based on the feedback you receive, don't ask for it. Soliciting opinions and then doing nothing is far worse than failing to ask in the first place. If they had some concerns before, they're really annoyed now.

"We'll exceed your expectations" is a cornball statement that fools no one... unless you can back it up by describing your firm's program to determine, measure and track client expectations and your action plan to respond to them. Set your firm apart from everyone else by telling your client how your process includes regular client feedback and maybe even a meeting specifically designed to identify and quantify their project expectations from which your team will establish goals and procedures to go beyond those goals by a measurable ten percent.

3. Admit when you're wrong

First, apologize. None of us particularly like being caught at our less-than-best. But letting your clients and colleagues see the less perfect side of you shows you to be real. It's especially important when you mess up (and who doesn't mess up periodically?) to 'fess up and admit your mistake. This gives you a credibility that you can never achieve by always claiming to be right or infallible. If they see that you're honest as you deal with mistakes, they will assume that you are honest in all your dealings.

Second, make it right. We all make mistakes. It's what you do after the mistake that separates the good from the great. While swallowing the big pill of remedying a mistake may seem tough at the time, the long term cost of not stepping up and doing the right thing is much greater. Compare the difference in public perception on two huge oil spills. After the Exxon Valdez incident, the company tried to deny wrongdoing and dodge responsibility, which resulted in a huge public relations mess. In contrast, when BP stepped in following the explosion in the Gulf of Mexico, we all criticized the original mistake, but gave the company full marks for their response.

4. Be price sensitive

No one is made of money and we all have to watch our budgets. While no one is asking you to slash your prices, be sensitive to your client's situation and be willing to take a smaller margin from a loyal client. Can you defer some scope items on a project until later so that they're able to go ahead with the project now?

Or why not take a lesson from the airlines? Do your frequent and loyal customers receive any type of discount on the price of their work? Can they earn 'points' that can be redeemed later on for an additional scope item or a small study? Loyalty programs are popular in many industries because they reward and lock-in customer allegiance. Since you're saving money on marketing with repeat customers, why not refund some of those savings in return for their loyalty?

5. Give back

Way back in kindergarten we all learned that, in order to receive, we have to be willing to give. In the adult world, we look for ways to give back to our friends and families, our communities, our alma maters and the environment.

Business development is all about looking for and asking for work. Relationships, on the other hand, are a two-way street that gives as well as receives. So before you ask your clients for another project, ask yourself what you've given to them lately. Do you have information on market trends that might be valuable? Do you have knowledge about new technologies or processes that they would find useful? Do you have a dozen donuts that they might enjoy?

6. Show your appreciation regularly

You can never say 'thank you' too many times. Your clients aren't just the source of your livelihood. Most of us enjoy friendships, professional relationships, mentoring and plain old good times with many of our clients. Make sure you express your gratitude for the friendships you enjoy, the assistance and guidance you are given, the revenue you depend on and the sustainability of your business because of the people with whom you work.

Your mother was right: don't forget to say 'thank you.'

How to lose a client

Way, way back, when I had my architectural practice, we had a client who was, by definition, perfect. He was a doctor for whom we successfully designed several medical clinics. What made him perfect? He never argued about fees and always paid his bills on time.

The fly in the ointment, however, was our differing personality styles. While I tend to be the classic extrovert, making quick decisions based largely on gut feel and having little patience for detail, he was an over-the-top analytical. Our project meetings would last the better part of a day and we'd cover the most excruciating details. He'd be analyzing yet another option for the color of the cover plates for the light switches and I'd be analyzing the option of jumping out of the 10th floor window.

Now, since I'm the one writing this account, I'm painting the extrovert as the more sensible approach. If the good doctor were relating the story, he'd likely have some choice words for what he felt was my shoddy attention to detail and my irresponsible decision-making. That's what makes relationships so entertaining.

Regardless of the assessment tool you use — Myers Briggs, DiSC profile or any other, there are four basic personality types separated by tendencies in both emotional and assertiveness levels.

The diagram looks like this:

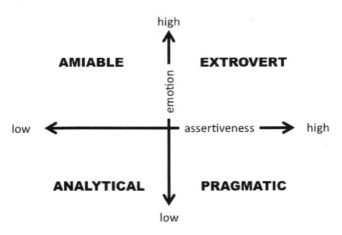

The relationship rule is that people on the same side of either of the lines tend to get along. The Extrovert and the Pragmatic get along because they agree that someone has to be in charge, so it might as well be me! The Pragmatic and the Analytical get along because they agree that, if we can remove all the emotional crap and just stick to the facts, everything will be fine. The Analytical and the Amiable get along because they both know that if we all just quiet down and stop the shouting, things will be easier. And the Amiable and the Extrovert get along because all that matters is whether or not you had a good time. Cuz life's too short to sweat the details.

We run into problems, however, with the diagonals. The Pragmatic tells his Amiable wife that he loves her on the day they get married and then wonders why she wants to hear the old news repeated every day. The Extrovert decides to buy the new car because he liked the color of one sitting at a stoplight while the Analytical needs a spreadsheet, two years worth of data and a complex algorithm to make the same decision.

Because my doctor client and I were diagonally opposite, we saw the world in very different ways and struggled to get along. Eventually the doctor and the work he brought us went away. He didn't go away mad, he just went away and didn't come back. I lost the client because I failed to properly manage his needs and preferences.

What might I have done differently? If I'd been smart enough, I could have asked someone else from the firm, whose personality style was more aligned with his, to manage the project. Or I could have 'pretended' to be an Analytical for the duration of our project meetings. But at the time I didn't know any of this and lost a perfectly good client as a result.

A good client manager must be somewhat of a chameleon and adapt themselves to that particular client's personality and preferences. That's not to say you're going develop multiple personalities, but rather lean in the direction and be empathetic to that client's tendencies. You might find they stick around longer.

Show your warts
We all know them. They're the sorts who, after they've dropped the ball, go to great lengths to assure us it wasn't their fault and deflect the blame to some other poor schmuck. The saddest thing about this kind of person is the utter transparency of their efforts. Usually, the fault is so obvious that their efforts to duck responsibility would be humorous if they weren't so despicable.

The one thing we all have in common with this poor sap is that we screw up. Regularly. And sometimes in a really big way. What separates us is what we do after we step in the doo-doo.

Who would you rather work with: The person who makes a mistake, then tells you why it wasn't really a mistake, why it doesn't matter and why it actually wasn't their fault? Or the person who comes to you, tells you they've made a mistake (often before you find out on your own) and tells you what they're going to do to fix it? Your clients would rather work with that person too.

When you try to hide a problem you've created or deflect the blame elsewhere, the trust that others have in you disappears. But when you step up and face the music, your credibility takes a huge leap. "If she's being honest with me about this, I've got to believe she's going to be honest with me about everything." It doesn't feel very good in the moment, but the long-term benefits are enormous.

Sure it's embarrassing to screw up. We all want to appear to be perfect and our egos take a big hit when we fall short of the mark. Our first instinct is to hide and hope no one notices. But then, when someone does notice, our second instinct is to make excuses or point the finger elsewhere. Every one of these actions simply digs the hole deeper, making it that much harder to climb out in the end. As much as it goes against your survival instincts, resist the temptation to duck, cover up or deflect. It makes you look like the two-year old who covers his eyes and thinks that nobody can see him.

Your client knows you're not infallible. They know you're going to make mistakes.

When you make that inevitable mistake, that's the time to show what you're really made of. Step up right away, tell the truth about what happened, then tell what you're going to do about it. It isn't that you screwed up. It's about what you do after it hits the fan.

When you mess up, 'fess up. This is a golden opportunity to set yourself truly apart from everyone else.

Exceeding Client Expectations

If I had a nickel for every time I've heard an AE firm tell a prospective client that they will "exceed your expectations" I'd be lying on a beach in Margaritaville.

It's a pretty common phrase and, on the surface, it makes sense. "Not only will we do what you expect, we'll go above and beyond and startle you with the quality of our work and service."

Nice sentiment, but there's a flaw in the argument: How can you exceed my expectations if you haven't found out what they are? And, while we're at it, exactly when and how do you determine that you've exceeded them and by how much? Because clients hear the phrase so often, and since no one ever inquires or follows up, they've come to see it for the trite drivel it is.

The idea of seeking out regular, reliable and candid feedback from clients is simultaneously exciting and terrifying. It feels great to get the "attaboys" and the glowing testimonials when things go well, but what kind of feedback do you want or get when you screw up? How often do you actively seek your clients' opinions about what you do well and what you do poorly? More importantly, what do you do with those opinions when they're given?

The first lesson in looking for client feedback is a word of caution. Regardless of how you learn what clients think, once they've shared their thoughts they fully expect you're going to do something about it. If you're not prepared to make real changes based on the feedback you receive, don't ask for it. Soliciting opinions and then doing nothing is far worse than failing to ask in the first place. If they had some concerns before, they're downright pissed now.

Informal Feedback

What's the best way to get honest and straightforward opinions? First, you should make it a regular habit to simply ask your clients for their candid views. No formal focus group session, just a quick question at the end of any (or every!) meeting.

How have we been doing lately?

Is there anything you'd like to see us improve?

How are we measuring up against (your competitor's name here) this year?

Continuous, informal feedback allows you to keep your finger on the pulse of your own performance and see how your image is fluctuating.

Formal Feedback

Firms are also finding big value in formally asking clients for their feedback. There are a variety of methods including one-on-one interviews, written or online surveys and focus groups. Each one has its advantages and drawbacks and you should experiment with different methods until you find one that works for you and your clients.

"We'll exceed your expectations" is a cornball statement that fools no one... unless you can back it up by describing your program to determine, measure and track client expectations and your action plan to respond to them. Set your firm apart by telling your client how your process includes regular client feedback and a project kickoff meeting to identify and quantify their expectations from which your team will establish goals and procedures to go beyond them by a measurable ten percent.

Now that's impressive.

9

MARKETING INFRASTRUCTURE

The Five Obligations of a Marketing Department

I believe that it's long past time for AE marketers to significantly raise their game. It's also way past time that Owners and Principals stand back and let their marketing team do the jobs they've been trained and hired for. Serious, sophisticated marketing strategies are required for a firm to grow and thrive today and most firms are falling far short of that mark.

Why? I see two problem areas. First, firm owners and principals somehow feel that they know more about marketing than the experts they've hired to do it for them. Just because you have a degree, a license and decades of experience as an engineer or architect does not mean you are an expert in how to sell those services. The bar of sophistication has gone way, way up and your ability to judge what's good and what works has not kept up.

Second, marketers are failing to show leadership and creativity in the role they play in their firms. Yes, I've heard all about how the boss won't let you. But it's your job to educate the boss and find a way. And that's simply not happening.

I believe that the marketing staff in every AE firm—whether that consists of a single individual or an entire team— has a set of responsibilities.

1. To Learn
They must remain lifelong students of marketing. Learn how marketing really works, not just in the AE industry but in all industries. Because the techniques we're using to sell AE services today were invented more than 100 years ago by the people who are still selling soap, cars and timeshare condos. And we need to catch up. We need to know what they know— the principles behind marketing, the psychology of persuasion. Study the masters—David Ogilvie, Al Ries, Jack Trout, Seth Godin, Jay Conrad Levinson. The list goes on. You can't sell something if you don't know how selling works.

2. To Stretch
Marketers must always be stretching, testing and experimenting with their ideas. When was the last time your firm tried something new and really different? Have you looked outside our industry to see what they're doing to sell other goods and services? Can you really call your marketing strategy 'creative?' Is it really any different from what the other guy is doing? When was the last time you tried something so different that you failed spectacularly and learned some really great lessons? What would your Super Bowl ad look like?

3. *To Question*

There is a lot of conventional wisdom surrounding AE marketing efforts. But is all of it right? Even if it did apply at one time, does it still apply? Is it really true that it's all about relationships? If so, how did the low-cost firm steal your long-term client? Is PowerPoint the answer to every presentation? Is CRM going to solve your cross-selling challenges? What if a lot of conventional wisdom was actually kinda stupid?

4. *To Guide*

When I was the VP of Sales and Marketing at a big construction company I made sure that every single day I would get out of my office and visit all the business unit leaders in the company. Sometimes I'd just stick my head in the door, sometimes it would be 15 minutes, sometimes we'd go to lunch. But every time I would use the opportunity to teach them something about marketing. "Here's what the marketing team is working on for you." "Here's what it's going to do for your business unit." "Here's the marketing principle that's behind it." After six months I had some really great partners who had a much better understanding of how marketing works.

5. *To Inspire*

This is a tough, competitive and high-stress business and it's easy to get down and cry the blues over just about everything. Somebody needs to maintain the sunny outlook and that should be the job of marketing. If anybody in the company ought to be capable of and responsible for high spirits, it's those who have been trained to be inherently optimistic and creative. We need a steady supply of optimism, enthusiasm and energy. I look to the Marketing Department for that infusion.

We spend so much time wringing our hands about how to differentiate one firm from the next. But the easiest and most powerful differentiator in the world would be a creative, energetic and sophisticated marketing strategy that put your company in front of a huge number of prospective clients over and over and over again. Who's going to have the nerve to be different?

Is your marketing department a trusted advisor?
So many firms aspire to 'trusted advisor' status with their clients. And so they should. A trust-based relationship speaks clearly to the value that you bring.

One of the hallmarks of this kind of rapport is that you regularly show your clients opportunities and possibilities that they may not have seen themselves. You bring them more than they expect to receive. It's the very definition of 'added value.'

What about the relationship between your firm and your Marketing Department?

In way too many instances, I see the marketing staff operating as a glorified secretarial pool. Proposal writing is an exercise in cut-and-paste and 'Save As.' Technical staff have the first and last say as proposals are edited and presentations are prepared, and the management team— with their architecture and engineering credentials—dictates what makes for good marketing.

This all-too-common approach misses out on an enormous opportunity and ignores the same kind of enlightened value that we try to sell to our clients.

If you've been smart in your hiring, the marketing team members who spend their days trying to help you win more work know a thing or two about marketing. They have at least a little (and sometimes a lot) of training and knowledge in marketing theory, writing, editing, graphic design and the vital art of persuasion. Yet far too many firms fail to take advantage of this great resource.

While it's true that you know your clients and their preferences best, it's not always true that you know the best way to communicate the value you can bring to them. There is an entire knowledge base and skill set that the vast majority of firm owners and technical staff simply don't possess. When your Marketing Department serves in that trusted advisor capacity, the collaboration between your knowledge of the client and their knowledge and skills in marketing, produce results that are far beyond your ability to achieve on your own.

Now, if you're a member of the marketing team and are smugly reading this, don't think that you're free of responsibility. One of the major reasons that firms don't treat their marketing staff as trusted advisors is because they've not been shown any reason for that trust.

You can't sell it if you don't understand it

When I stepped into the VP of Marketing role at the construction company, I inherited a marketing staff of seven. It was a talented group. Impressive writers, graphic designers, editors and marketing theorists, but...

One afternoon, the lead proposal writer came into my office

and asked, in a sincere and completely un-ironic way, "What is design-build?"

With my jaw on the floor I realized that, as great as this team was at marketing, they had no idea what we were selling.

The company had seven Divisions including hospitals, industrial plants, retail developments, airports and interior fit-ups, all depending on my team to show them in the best possible light. How could I expect the head of the healthcare group to trust one of my team to write a great proposal for the next hospital project if they didn't even understand a simple construction concept like design build?

The next morning I outfitted the entire team with hard hats and work boots and we started our construction education. We made regular visits to the job sites, sat in on job meetings and bought the donuts and coffee for the weekly Superintendent's meeting. We watched pile driving, concrete pours and sheet rock installation. They learned about subcontractor coordination and the life-and-death importance of controlling dust when you're renovating a neo-natal intensive care unit.

In short, they got their boots dirty and their eyes full of exactly what the company got paid to do and what they were helping to sell.

The immersion course lasted for about a month, but the education didn't stop there. Although we backed off a bit from the initial intensity, we maintained weekly site visits and regular conversations with the estimating and preconstruction teams.

The results were as staggering as the initial shock had been. Their level of understanding of the content of the proposals they were writing shot up and it allowed them to communicate the value the company provide far more compellingly. They had a whole new facility with the language of construction and our hit rate went up.

But the biggest benefit was the new level of communication between the technical folks and the marketing team. They'd won some admirers when they showed up for the 5AM meetings in their work boots and the job-hardened construction pros gave them a whole new level of respect.

Don't misinterpret. This does NOT mean that everyone on your marketing team ought to be engineers, architects or otherwise have some technical background. I get that reaction frequently when the technical folks roll their eyes if the new Head of Marketing didn't come with a P.E. or AIA after their name.

In fact, I often shy away from the technical-professional-turned-marketer because they frequently don't have the communication skills that are necessary. Tough as this may sound, it's usually a lot easier to teach a marketer enough about design or construction than it is to teach a technical professional how to communicate persuasively.

How much does your marketing team know about what your firm does? How often are they out at a job site? Have they ever sat through a tough project management meeting and seen what goes on? Can they talk the talk?

You can't sell what you don't understand.

Staffing Your Marketing Effort

I frequently encounter a lot of resistance when I'm talking to design firm leaders about staffing up for their marketing efforts. The fear, of course, is that increased overhead costs reduce a firm's competitiveness and economic viability. Nobody seems to mind the overhead that accounting or administrative staff adds, but marketing staff is proverbially that horse of a different color.

I have as much respect for the dreaded Overhead Ogre as the next guy. But reasonable and intelligent overheads, carefully invested, provide tremendous returns. Likewise, failure to invest in appropriate overheads can bite you where it hurts. Fail to invest in properly trained and skilled marketing staff and you'll leave a nasty scar.

I don't know where it comes from but there seems to be a general belief among design professions that marketing tasks such as writing, graphic design, proposal preparation, etc., are relatively straightforward and capable of being accomplished by anyone with a reasonable command of the English language. Not so!

I regularly see highly trained and talented design professionals making bad marketing decisions because they have no training or background in this complex discipline. They cost their firms countless dollars in wasted efforts while failing to achieve the wins they want.

Here's what you should do:

Step 1 – Invest in one full time, trained and qualified marketing staff member for every 25 technical staff. Your first hire should be a Marketing Coordinator with a marketing, journalism or advertising background and at least five year's experience. Your second hire should be a Junior Marketing Coordinator who can free the first hire from the more routine tasks so he or she can focus on higher-level strategies.

Step 2 – Listen carefully to what they say and seriously consider taking their advice.

As with becoming a skilled and knowledgeable engineer or architect, it takes a particular combination of training and talent to be an effective marketer. There is a body of knowledge and a set of skills that only come with the investment of much time and effort. Your client hires you because you bring knowledge and skills that they don't possess. If your client tried to design the bridge, the building, or the treatment plant without your expert input, the results would be disastrous.

The same is true when trained architects and engineers assume they can do their own marketing. Yes, there are some basic tasks that can be done successfully, but I regularly see people without training and experience making critical decisions that are just plain wrong. Not only are the marketing results bad, it's a waste of the engineering and design talent. Let's put the square pegs into the square holes and benefit from the highest and best use of everyone's time and talents.

It's not only a mistake, it's a waste of time and money to assume that someone with extensive training and experience as an engineer or architect would be able to step up and be effective as a copy writer or graphic designer. The best people to execute your marketing are those trained and skilled in marketing.

The lights you turn on, the chair you sit in and the coffee you drink to get you rolling in the morning are all overhead costs. Your client's investment in your fees is nothing but overhead in their operation. If you want your marketing to be successful it's absolutely essential to invest in trained, qualified marketing professionals.

The Strawberry Jam Theory

Marketing resources are like strawberry jam—the farther you spread them, the thinner they get. And if you're anything like me, a thin, barely visible skim of jam on your toast just won't cut it.

One of the most pervasive challenges I see among marketing folks around the country is the tendency to spread themselves too thin. Proposal writing, brand building, press releases, business development coordination... Oh, and can you please speak to this person asking for a donation for the local high school booster club? That's marketing, isn't it?

If it seems too often that you're only barely managing to stay a step ahead of the freight train that's bearing down on you, it might be worthwhile to rethink your approach. Operating in reactive mode all the time gives you no opportunity to plan, strategize or reflect on where you've been or are heading.

So is the solution to have more jam or less toast? We all work with a finite supply of resources—time, money, staff—but there are ways to leverage the resources you do have to make them more effective. Here are some tips I've found useful:

Prioritize: Take a look at your marketing plan. (You have one, right?) Then ask yourself, "What's the ONE THING I could be spending my time on that will take us to those objectives the fastest?" Then devote at least 50% of your time to this task. Everything else is secondary and can wait. If you don't have a marketing plan, maybe preparing one is your ONE THING.

Focus: We often spend more time switching between tasks than we do working on the tasks themselves. Instead of launching a Facebook page, an internal newsletter, a PR campaign and an update of your resume library, pick one. A really good job done on just one will bring you far more benefit than a poor or half-finished job on all four.

Outsource: While you're the only one who can do certain marketing and business development tasks, there are many that can be done by freelance experts on a contract basis. Market research, development of your contact list, graphic design, template building, writing, editing and staff training are just some of the functions that can be easily, effectively and economically outsourced.

Bring in Interns: While I'm vigorously opposed to the practice of getting student interns to work for free, I'm a big fan of bringing in these energetic, enthusiastic and low-cost staffers to work on one-time projects. With just a little coaching and management, they're naturals for organizing your photo library, researching that new market you've been contemplating, updating resumes or tackling that huge pile of yet-to-be-filed proposals.

Each of these tactics will make your jam go a little farther while still retaining that sweet strawberry taste.

If you're not a jam fan, here's another way to think about it: Imagine that you're an Army General heading into a battle with 5,000 troops. Would you string your soldiers out in a line, 5,000 men long and one man deep and say, 'Charge!?' Of course not. It would be suicide. Instead you'd concentrate your troops and focus on a small number of key targets. Once that high ground was secured, you'd regroup and then aim for the next strategic objectives.

If you're going to execute a marketing strategy, make the effort worthwhile. You'll get far more benefit from one really well-executed initiative than from five ideas that are only half-baked.

Measuring Your Marketing ROI

Many CEO's and CFO's are asking hard questions of their marketing teams regarding the spending of scarce dollars in the effort to win new work. And so they should! As much as the marketers might squirm under the spotlight, the questions are legitimate and need to be asked. If spending can't be justified with a clear return it should be cut off.

That said, it's extremely hard to measure marketing ROI in any business because it's often impossible to credit a particular sale to a particular marketing effort.

In some cases it's easy. If you were a mattress company offers a '4th of July Special' and sales go up over the holiday weekend, it's pretty clear-cut. Likewise, if they put a big push on advertising in a certain region and sales go up in that area, we can credit the promotion. The calculation becomes an easy one of dividing total sales by the cost of the advertising campaign.

But when Coca Cola puts a billboard by the side of the highway, they don't even try to measure how many additional cans of Coke they sell. It's enough to know that every person driving past that sign is a potential Coke drinker and, if they didn't put a sign there, Pepsi would. So if measuring marketing ROI is challenging in business in general, it's even more challenging in the AE business.

It's very difficult to credit a particular project win to a particular marketing tactic. That new client may have first heard of your firm from an award you won, then learned more about you through your email blast program, been impressed as one of your team members spoke at a conference, then made the final decision when your well-written proposal was competitively priced. While each of these initiatives contributed, it's impossible to allocate precise percentages of effort that resulted in the win.

It's also difficult to compare your results with industry standards because 'industry standards' are, at best, some rough rules of thumb. The AE industry represents a relatively small sector of the overall business world and collecting meaningful data is a real challenge. Those that try to survey the profession face very small sampling sizes and inconsistent tracking methods.

Now, having told you how difficult, if not impossible this effort is, let me go on to give you some very clear guidelines that will help you get the most from your marketing dollars and measure your return.

Way back in Chapter 3 we talked about the concept of the 'Marketing Racetrack.' Instead of thinking about marketing as one non-stop endeavor, the 'win work' effort should be viewed as a series of consecutive steps that ultimately lead to a new client and then ensure they stick around in a long-term relationship.

While your ultimate goal is a client with signed contracts, not each of these steps will produce that result. Your return on a brand-building effort, for example, shouldn't be measured by the number of new projects you sign in a year. Each step has its own clear goals and your measurements should focus on how well you achieved that goal.

ROI in the Positioning Phase

Measuring ROI on marketing planning is tricky. But the most fundamental and best thing you can do is answer two simple questions:

1. Do we have a detailed marketing plan for the next 12-24 months?

2. Are we executing the elements of that plan in accordance with the schedule we established?

If you answer 'no' to either or both of those questions, you are getting a very poor return on your planning effort. You invested the effort and now you're doing nothing about it. ROI doesn't get lower than that.

If you answer 'yes' to both those questions, you WILL be achieving a high return on your planning investment. You WILL be making a positive impression in those markets and you WILL see results.

- 14% of firms have no marketing plan at all
- Of those that do, less than half include a firm-wide budget in the plan
- Only half update their plan at least annually

ROI on Branding

Since the goal of brand building is to raise the knowledge and understanding of your firm throughout your market, the best way to measure the effectiveness of the effort is to conduct regular surveys of the market to see how much that knowledge has been raised.

A simple perception survey, conducted annually, will provide clear data on the results of your campaign. If perception and understanding is going up, your efforts are working.

Measuring ROI is also a simple matter. Most firms obtain between 70% and 90% of their revenue from repeat clients. Presumably, those clients don't come back because of your brand building efforts. They already know the firm.

By tracking new client activity, and making a point to determine how the new clients first heard about the firm, you can gauge the return on your branding investment. If you spend $25,000 in a year for brand building and it attracts one new client with a $50,000 project, your ROI is 200% in the first year. If that client sticks around with additional projects, your ROI goes higher still.

- Half of the firms report that they get qualified leads from their website. Of those, more than 80% turn into paying projects

- 65% have offered seminar workshops for clients and report that they average three leads per workshop.

- Half of the firms report that they participate in trade shows. 85% find it worthwhile and generate 4-8 leads per event. 95% say it increases visibility. 89% say it builds relationships

ROI on Business Development
This is another tricky one. We know that this is a relationship-based business and that friends like to work with friends. But there are so many other variables involved in winning work that it's difficult to isolate the relationship-building component and measure its contribution.

That doesn't mean we shouldn't try and there are a number of metrics that are indicative of strong, trust-based client relationships. These measures will give you a good indicator of the success of your BD activities.

- Percentage of sole-source, or qualifications-based work
- Ease of fee negotiations
- Number of project opportunities

- 36% of firms have paid, full-time business development representatives
- 77% have a 4-year degree, but only 40% are technical
- Less than a quarter are registered professionals

Maximizing your ROI on Proposals and Presentations
The ROI calculation on your proposals and presentation investments is simple:

$$ROI = \frac{\text{total revenue from projects won through proposals}}{\text{proposal costs}}$$

By far, the biggest ROI you can achieve is from a rigorous and disciplined Go/No Go decision-making process.

You can double your hit rate by simply cutting in half the number of proposals you submit. You can prove this by running the above calculation again, but this time insert a number for proposal cost that is just half the previous number. Your ROI will double.

- Only 17% of firms always conduct a go/no go
- Average hit rate is between 25% and 30%

ROI on Customer Service
The investment you make in high quality customer service will have a direct impact on the amount of repeat work, the ease of contract negotiations and the number of referrals to new clients that are provided by existing clients.

No one really knows how much more it costs to land a new client than keep an existing one. But we know it's more.

- Most firms get between 70% and 90% of their work from repeat clients
- 70% is too few. Why aren't more clients coming back?
- 90% is too many. There are too many eggs in too few baskets and not enough fresh clients coming in

Marketing Budgets

Every firm wants to know how much it should be spending on marketing. And in the pursuit of that answer, they look to see how much other firms are spending. Determining that statistic is proving to be impossible.

First, the design professions are a relatively small industry in comparison to the world of business in general. So not many people are paying attention to the numbers. Second, those that are trying to survey such things run into very small sample sizes and inconsistent reporting.

For example, the most recent Marketing Survey conducted by The Zweig Group had only 106 respondents. While Zweig does its best to work with these numbers and make them relevant, it's hard to draw reliable conclusions from such a small sample spread over small, medium and large firms serving who-knows-how-many different markets.

Nonetheless, between these statistics and the anecdotal evidence that we see throughout the industry, it's possible to reach some conclusions.

- Less than half of firms prepare a marketing budget

- Those that do, plan to spend about 3.5% of net service revenue* on all marketing activities

- Those that track their spending find that they spend a little more than 5% of net service revenue

Without getting into the detail of upper and lower quartiles and medians versus means, here's how that spending tends to break down.

(Keep in mind that these numbers are derived from a combination of industry statistics, anecdotal evidence and a bit of guesswork. But that's the best we've got.)

Marketing Staff Labor	35%
Other Marketing Labor	14% - 20%
Proposals	5% - 15%
Client Entertainment	4% - 6%
Travel	2% - 6%
Brand Building Activities	7% - 14%

Now, to compare and put this into perspective, the average small business marketing budget is 9-12% of business revenue. So, to the degree that we can trust the numbers, the average AE firm is spending less than half on marketing as their regular, small business counterpart.

If your firm is one of the more than half that does not prepare a marketing budget, it's time to start working on that. But don't fire up the spreadsheet just yet. It's going to take you at least two years of tracking your expenditures before you are able to develop a marketing budget that has any useful accuracy.

So don't try to develop a budget yet. Just keep careful track of what you are spending, do some rudimentary ROI calculations and work towards being able to set goals for both spending and ROI in the future.

As you allocate spending, put about 80% of your budget towards retaining and growing your existing clients. Spend 20% to find new ones.

If you want to grow, expand into a new region or market sector, you're going to have to increase your marketing investment. If you're driving a car at 30 mph and you want to accelerate to 60, you have to burn some gas. Once you're up to the higher speed, you can back off on the accelerator and 'cruise' along the highway. So increase your marketing budget in growth years. Decrease it in times of 'status quo.'

*   *Net service revenue is your total revenue, minus pass-through fees to other consultants and reimbursable expenses*

Measuring your marketing success

We all learned some tough fiscal lessons from the Great Recession. One of them is that we need to constantly ask if we're getting a good return on our various investments. In the marketing arena, firm owners are asking hard questions about the spending of scarce dollars in the effort to win new work. Good for them!

That said, marketing ROI is a slippery pig to grab hold of since it's hard to assign clear credit to any particular undertaking. That new client may have first heard of your firm from an award you won, then learned more about you through your email blast program, been impressed as one of your team members spoke at a conference, then made the final decision when your well-written proposal was competitively priced. While each of these initiatives contributed, it's impossible to allocate precise percentages of effort that resulted in the win.

There's an old saying in the ad business: "Fifty percent of all advertising works. We just don't know which half." While I know more than a few engineers whose hair might catch on fire from this notion, there are some very clear guidelines that will help you get the most from your marketing dollars and useful ways to measure your return. Here are the four measures that I like to use:

1. Do you have a marketing plan and is it being executed on schedule? If you have a solid marketing plan and it's being rolled out relatively close to schedule, you WILL see results from your efforts. The results will vary and come from different sources that are too diverse to be worth the effort to track individually. Think of it like a fitness program – if you're eating properly and exercising daily, you are getting more fit, whether you weigh yourself every day or not.

2. Is 'brand awareness' increasing as measured by client surveys? The best client survey device I know of comes from a company in North Carolina called Design Facilitator. www.designfacilitator.com I have no problem blatantly

plugging a product that works well and I highly recommend it.

3. Are you receiving positive, informal feedback? Your senior executives, project managers and business developers ought to be seeking regular feedback from clients in their day-to-day engagements. A simple, 'How are we doing lately?' or 'Is there anything we could be doing to improve our service to you?' at every encounter will give you plenty of informal feedback. Don't worry too much about recording this feedback, but talk about it regularly and take it seriously.

4. Are your hit rates increasing? This includes click rates on your web site and win rates on your proposals and interviews. These should be tracked carefully and you ought to be seeing steady and regular improvement.

There you have it—four areas to measure and only two of them produce actual numbers. While the left-brainers in the crowd might yearn for something a little more calibrated, I firmly believe that these will produce all the measurement you need. Beyond that, any tracking efforts are more trouble than they're worth. Spend your time and resources on the effort of marketing and the score-keeping will be easy.

10

THE CENTER OF THE UNIVERSE

Throughout this book we've repeated again and again that nothing matters except what your client wants. I've spoken about how everyone shares the same favorite subject: themselves. And how you must always build your entire sales effort by first crawling inside your client's head to see what the world looks like from that vantage point.

This approach has always been important. But as we find our way in this post-recession world, it's more critical than ever.

So it makes sense that we allow your clients to have the last word in this book. Over the years we've collected comments from your clients. They come from formal debriefings, comments made during interviews and casual conversations. They provide invaluable insight into what goes on in those important heads. So pay attention.

1.   We Lost

This is a memo sent by the Marketing Director of a construction firm following their team's loss on an interview.

Re: recent presentation.

Comments from client:

- *No one showed enthusiasm*
- *I understand that superintendents and field staff might not be the best speakers, but the rest of the team showed no enthusiasm at all.*
- *It really affects how we react to you.*

Prior to the presentation, we were all in the room getting ready and waiting for the client to arrive. The client's Head of Facilities walked in and our guys were so focused on what they were going to say, that they never even got up to say 'hello.'

We lost.

2.   Who's Excited?

This is the text of a memo from a Business Development representative of an engineering firm. The firm was getting ready for an upcoming interview and the BD rep was relating a (rare and valuable) conversation he'd just had with the head of the selection committee. (Names have been changed.)

Hello Folks,

I wanted to pass onto you all a conservation I had with Susan Lee today. Susan is the Director of the Engineering Department and on the selection committee. I was advised not to ask her about the project from someone close to her but I had to call her regarding a grant we were helping the city and a local non-profit with. At the end of the conservation she asked me if there was any information I needed for the Flood Study. Well, I was prepared and below are my notes verbatim.

1. *"All the remaining firms are strong technically. They are all about equal so what it will come down to is who are the folks that are really excited about the project, who really want to do the work, and who do we (being the city) feel we will be able to work with the best".*

2. *When asked if she likes one central presenter or the entire team, she responded with the following. What makes our team strong is the team itself. Therefore she personally would like to hear from the different team members but mentioned that we should not have any team members present who are "overbearing" or that are strong technically but will not connect with the selection committee. If any of the speakers are "technically dry" do not have them present.*

3. *Also make sure the team is well organized so the transitions between speakers are smooth and fluid. Avoid distractions during the transitions. All speakers need to stay on point and connect with the committee.*

4. *So it seems that we will want to work towards making a strong connection with them, be enthusiastic with good energy, and have all the speakers make sure that they are not "technically dry". Basically we want them to like us.*

Thanks and I hope this is helpful.

Bill

5. Are they the sort of people you want to work with?

This is an evaluation checklist used by a client organization when reviewing submittals and interviews by consultants. It asks two very pertinent questions that your business marketing effort must answer. At the end of the day, when your branding has done its work, your business developers have gone home, your proposal has been read and you've completed your presentation, how would <u>your</u> client answer these questions?

1. *When reading about how the firm is going to handle your current project, are you acutely aware of the benefits this firm will bring you? Is it apparent this firm is different from all the others you've reviewed? Is their approach to solving your problem clear and sensible? Are you left with a high level of confidence this firm can handle the project without any difficulty?*

2. *When learning about the project team and its individual members, do you feel you are getting to know them personally? Are you convinced they can do the job? Do they seem like the sort of people you would want to work with on all of your projects? Are you anxious to work with them?*

There you have it: an entire book summed up beautifully in just a few points by someone other than the authors. We couldn't have said it better ourselves.

Now it's your turn to get out there and knock 'em dead!

ABOUT THE AUTHORS

DAVID A. STONE

Trained as an architect, David Stone has launched three companies and has helped countless engineers, design professionals and marketers craft their strategies, shape their proposals and win a steady supply of profitable work. He is the author of 17 books, a much sought-after presenter and keynote speaker at gatherings around the world, and a trusted advisor to CEOs and Presidents of engineering and architecture firms in every region of the U.S.

GAIL HULNICK

Gail Hulnick holds an M.B.A. in Marketing, an MA in Journalism, and an M.F.A. in Creative Writing. Her background includes many years as the host of her own radio show and as a television news reporter and anchor. Through her company, WindWord Communications, she has coached thousands of business and professional people in presentation and media skills. In 2015, she and David started blüStone Marketing to provide high-level coaching and education for marketing AE services.

ABOUT BLÜSTONE MARKETING

Based in Savannah, Georgia and Vancouver, B.C., blüStone's mission is to guide AE firms toward the stategies and practices that will earn them a steady supply of profitable work.

ABOUT OUR MARKETING LIBRARY

Please visit our website at www.blustonemarketing.com

You'll find an extensive library of books, recorded webinars, and Ebooks., as well as a comprehensive, marketing system called *Winning Work.*

News of our upcoming live webinars, appearances at association meetings, and keynote presentations can be found on the website and on our social media channels: Twitter, Facebook, Google + and YouTube.

Made in the USA
Columbia, SC
02 December 2018

To my brother, who made me want to be a ballplayer
from the very beginning